D1496489

I have known Dr. Joe Cannon, both personally and professionally, for over 25 years. Joe is a special veterinarian who not only possesses knowledge and experience, but has a genuine interest and a sincere caring for all animals, especially exotics.

I have seen him in action, be it in the middle of the night or coming in on his day off to care for one of his charges.

The stories told in this book are true-life adventures of a modern-day "Doc Tari." To this day I continue to call on Joe for his knowledge of exotic animals that need his help.

This is a great read for anyone who cares about these wonderful creatures.

Mickey Hunt
exotic animal expert and
Vice President of International Wildlife, Ltd.

Dr. Joe Cannon's accounts of his vast experiences with all kinds of animals, from pets to exotic wildlife, provide a heartwarming, enlightening, and sometimes terrifying story of his lifetime as an animal lover and veterinarian. If you are an animal lover too, you will love reading about his encounters with these creatures that have brought so much joy and meaning to his life. The lessons learned and so fascinatingly related by Dr. Cannon surely demonstrate that animals can make better human beings out of us all.

Charles E. Bates
retired editor and journalism teacher

SAFARI DOCTOR

Life and Adventures of a
Texas Wildlife Park
Veterinarian

Dr. Joe Cannon

Path Publishing

Amarillo, Texas

First edition 2006

For marketing and publishing issues:
Path Publishing, Inc.
4302 W. 51st #121
Amarillo, Texas 79109-6159
USA
path2@pathpublishing.com

To order copies and contact the author:
LP Fulfillment Services
P. O. Box 20454
Amarillo, Texas 79114-2454
USA
safari.cannon@gmail.com

Cover and interior design by
Cathleen Baldauf, Amarillo, Texas
cathleen.baldauf@gmail.com

ISBN 978-1-891774-05-8
ISBN 1-891774-05-0
LCCN 2005909843

Printed in the United States of America

CONTENTS

In Memory

This book is dedicated to the memory of my parents, Bryce Russell Cannon and Margaret Adelle Cannon, who sacrificed many things during their lives so I might have the opportunity to follow my dreams. Their love and wisdom provided an environment that allowed me the freedom to think, to feel, and to follow my natural instincts concerning my life and my future.

PROLOGUE

Many young boys and girls probably dream of growing up on a farm, having all kinds of wild animals as pets, and of one day becoming a veterinarian. Since everyone's goal is to spend their life doing something they really enjoy, it would be a dream come true for someone who enjoys and loves animals to spend their life treating and caring for the very creatures they love so much.

This book is a collection of my memoirs. I am very grateful for having been able to live my dreams. My life began on an 80-acre farm near a small Texas community called Greens Creek, about two hours south of Dallas. The farm was the home of just about every animal you could imagine. Many wild animals and birds also called Greens Creek their home. It was my interaction with farm animals and wild pets that helped me decide to become a veterinarian in the late 1950s. I received excellent training, having graduated from Texas A&M University School of Veterinary Medicine in 1969 and completing an internship at the University of California-Davis in 1970-1971. Over the next 35 years of my career, the most enjoyable part of my practice turned out to be the time spent at International Wildlife Park-Grand Prairie, Texas, where I held the position of resident veterinarian from 1972-1984.

In these chapters you will meet unforgettable animal characters: Silky Harris the fox, Red the hawk, Damien the African elephant, Ellie the orphan elk, Squeaky the cheetah, Judy the chimp from *Daktari*, Dudley the blackbuck antelope, Big Daddy the killer hippo, Werewolf the ugly lion, Football the baby rhino, and many more. You also will travel along on wild animal captures and immobilizations, including a trip to Mexico.

Some stories are warm, some are amusing, and some are downright scary, but the one thing they all have in common is that they are about animals, their behavior, and their wonderful interactions with man. It is with the utmost admiration for all of these magnificent creatures that this book was written, and with the hope that you, the reader, will come away with a better understanding and appreciation for how God's creatures interact with man, as well as themselves.

INTRODUCTION

From my earliest childhood memories of growing up on a farm, I always have been compelled to spend my time with animals. Fish, fowl, or mammals continually have held a fascination for me, and I have never considered doing anything other than having a life and career centered on animals. The events in this book are priceless memories to me, as I have had experiences in the animal world that money cannot buy. These experiences have served to greatly increase my respect for the strength and intelligence of all of God's creatures.

The part of my life that I devoted to exotic animals was totally unexpected but turned out to be the most rewarding and memorable. It is ironic how life sometimes works out that way. I do know that my two pets on the farm, Silky the fox and Red the hawk, both played major roles in the development of my philosophy of life, and they were strong influences on me during my formative years. It was only a short time after my graduation from veterinary school that exotics popped back into my life.

While I was attending the University of California at Davis on an ambulatory equine internship, part of my coursework was making weekly rounds at the Sacramento Zoo. It was there that I met Dr. Murry Fowler, the professor supervising our rounds at the zoo, and he reawakened my interest in exotics. He had been on staff at UC-Davis for several years and was one of the pioneers in exotic animal medicine. He later published the textbook and bible for exotic medicine, *Zoo and Wild Animal Medicine*. I was extremely fortunate to have worked with him since his knowledge and understanding of exotics was unequaled during that time.

Dr. Fowler taught me a great deal about chemical immobilization, which is a must in the handling of wild animals. Being able to examine tranquilized animals opened up a whole new dimension for me. As it turned out, I would become a pioneer in the use of M-99 (etorphine, a synthetic cousin of morphine and much more effective), and between 1973 and 1984 I used more M-99 for the capture of wild animals than anyone else in the United States. Dr. Fowler, my mentor, taught me well in the science of chemical restraint, enabling me to perform examinations, diagnostics, surgery, preventive medicine, and more.

As I began to handle, examine, and treat these amazing animals, I found that they quickly became part of my life. I learned that when a wild animal begins to appear ill, it is usually too late to do much. Why? The adrenalin rush and endorphin release that all wild animals possess allows them to keep going in the face of severe illness. Only when the infection or disease begins to finally take over the body do they begin to get weak or stop eating. By that time, the animal may be almost dead. That's why I started to watch for earlier and more subtle signs of illness, using chemical immobilization if I suspected a problem. I could then draw blood, do an exam, and start treatment before the disease reached its final stages.

In 1971, I became the resident veterinarian for Earl Scheib's Green Thumb Thoroughbred Farm in Chino, California. While there, I was invited by a close friend to visit him at the Lion Country Safari in nearby Laguna Hills, which was the first park in California to attempt the open, drive-through concept in which visitors were caged in cars while the wild animals roamed around them. I enjoyed my visits so much that I volunteered my services and worked almost every weekend.

Every effort was made to make the park as similar to Africa as possible, with four separate compounds housing different species of animals that ran free in each. The lions and cheetahs were allowed to roam in their designated areas, and groups of giraffe, wildebeest, zebra, rhino, eland, and impala shared common areas.

The concept was wonderful! To see these magnificent creatures in a natural setting, where they could roam free and interact with each other, seemed to be the answer to conservation, display, and breeding all rolled into one.

During my one-year volunteer period at the wildlife park, I came to realize that exotics were special to me and that I wanted to dedicate a large portion of my veterinary practice to maintaining their health and happiness. I wanted to learn more about their habits and behavior, and become proficient in all aspects of their care.

With this in the back of my mind, my ears perked up when I heard of a new wildlife park opening up in Grand Prairie, Texas, just west of Dallas. Pat Quinn, the director of the Laguna Hills Park, had mentioned for some time that this was a possibility, but it was not until I asked him directly did he acknowledge that it was definite and that construction had already begun. I told Pat I would be very interested in becoming the resident veterinarian there, especially since I was originally from that area of Texas. He said he would put in a good word for me, and we left it at that.

About six months later I was offered the job. I couldn't have been happier, as this would not only give my family an opportunity to get back home, but also allow me to use the park as a foundation to start my own veterinary practice in Grand Prairie. With a great deal of anticipation, my family and I started back to Texas to begin what would turn out to be the most exciting 12 years of my life.

The park, soon to be completed, was owned by International Animal Exchange. With their headquarters in Michigan, they were the largest importers and exporters of exotic animals in the world. Wildlife conservation and preservation were their main goals. They owned and operated the Mount Kenya Game Preserve for many years. Working closely with the actor William Holden, they accomplished many breeding and wildlife relocation programs for numerous species of endangered animals in this park. It was their hope that through the creation of a large wildlife park in America, even more captive breeding programs could be established worldwide.

Brian, Don, Tom, and Mickey Hunt, the owners and operators of International Animal Exchange, were true pioneers in wildlife conservation. Their plan for captive breeding programs included many species of exotics, such as Bongo antelope, Arabian oryx, Gaur cattle, Barasingha deer, white zebra, and white tigers.

Mickey Hunt was appointed Vice President and General Manager to supervise all of these projects. He would ultimately become my boss and confidant. Today, he is Vice President of International Wildlife, Ltd.

The park's 360 lush acres were bound by the Trinity River and divided into five compounds, one more than Laguna Hills. Section I was hoof stock, containing some two hundred head of various African, antelope-type animals; in addition, this section included the main watering holes that had large islands in the middle where chimpanzees and other species of primates were housed. Section II was home to the African lions, with some prides as large as 20 to 30 animals. Section III housed rhinos, hippos, cheetah, and Cape buffalo, and also contained several lakes with islands

13

that served as the home for spider monkeys and chimpanzees. In Section IV were the elephants, along with several species of hoof stock, including giraffe. Section V was the River Ride, home to many species of deer, birds, small primates, and some moated carnivores such as wolves, hyenas, and bears. Near the River Ride was the hospital nursery facility, which also housed some reptiles, birds, and small mammals.

For the next 10 years I devoted a large part of my life to caring for these wonderful wild animals. I will always consider it a great honor for them to have allowed me into their world. The park rangers and directors, who were an integral part of the day-to-day operation of this huge facility and are equally unforgettable, included characters such as Bill York, George Gray, James Ashe, Mickey Hunt, John Clay, Craig Collvins, Kurt Giesler, Vern McGran, Ron Surratt, and Ray Sutton. It is with special thanks and honor to them that I write this book. As you roam through the chapters, I hope you find these stories as fascinating as I do. International Wildlife Park-Grand Prairie ultimately closed for business after two major floods, but the animals will live forever in my heart. Enjoy!

CHAPTER 1

SILKY HARRIS

Life on a farm in the little community of Greens Creek was simple and peaceful. Greens Creek was named after the creek that ran through it. I spent a lot of time on this creek hunting, fishing and just being a boy. My dad had to work long hours, what with farming more than one hundred acres of dry-land peanuts and tending to the livestock. There wasn't much time for fun or play on the farm. I had to grab that time when I could, because Mom and Dad always managed to find some work for me to do.

As far back as I can remember, my day on the farm began at daylight with feeding the livestock, which included cattle, sheep, hogs, chickens, and at times, maybe a horse or two. Tending to the animals was my favorite chore. I think they liked me as well as I liked them.

When the feeding was done, I went back to the house for a hearty breakfast of water biscuits, water gravy, sugar syrup, and sometimes ham or bacon, if we had recently butchered a hog. After breakfast, it was off to the fields to work all morning, either plowing or hoeing peanuts, our cash crop. We would rest for a little while after lunch and then go back to the fields to work at what we had been doing that morning. In the evenings, my relaxing hot bath consisted of water being heated on the stove in a pan and poured into a porcelain tub. This usually gave me about two or three inches of water to sit in, and that was after repeating the heating process two or three times.

As my dad always said though, "It sure beats nothin'." We simply couldn't afford indoor plumbing.

I didn't understand what Mom and Dad were talking about when they would say, "Times are hard." I remember they talked a lot about money or the lack of it, and sometimes Dad would laugh and say, "We're so poor that the poor sneer at us."

One reason I never realized how poor we were was because we ate good. We always had vegetables such as black-eyed peas, green beans, potatoes, squash, okra, and tomatoes that we grew in our garden. We usually had home-raised beef, pork, and chicken, besides the wild game I brought home from my hunting. The wild game might be venison, quail, squirrel, duck, or a rabbit now and then. So, in a nutshell, I ate good, worked hard, slept good at night, and learned to despise our outhouse and lack of indoor bathroom plumbing. Getting friends to come spend the night was pretty tough.

At times I have mixed emotions about how I grew up. When I think back on those "hard times" and how hard we had to work, I feel sort of cheated in the fun department. On the other hand, I feel so fortunate that I grew up in the country where I had clean air to breathe, parents who loved me, a warm place to sleep, good home-cooked meals to eat, and a chance to bond with a host of animal friends.

I managed to have a few pets of my own to keep me company. They included the usual dogs and cats, but that never seemed to be enough for me. It seemed that the more that I was around animals, the more I wanted to understand everything about them. I was curious about all animals and especially wildlife. This probably explains why I adopted squirrels, crows, hawks, owls, and foxes. Dad didn't have much patience with these unusual pets, but Mom was very understanding about them. I think she realized that sometimes life on a farm could be lonely without pets. She even helped with my feeding formulas and would go out with me on some of my jaunts from time to time. I enjoyed those times. I believe God put animals on this earth so that we could learn such things as patience, responsibility, love and nurturing from them. They probably taught me more about life than my parents and peers.

I lived to have a day off, due to a rain or a broken piece of farming equipment. This gave me some free time to hit the woods and fields to explore or hunt for food. I pretty much had to make my own amusement since we lived so far "out in the sticks." It was on one of these rainy days when the sun had popped out, but was still too wet to plow or hoe in the fields, that my cousin, Bill Bamber, showed up. He knew I would not be working, and he was looking for a hunting partner.

"Hey, Cuz," he yelled as he walked up the road to our house. "Let's go over behind the old Henson woods and look around."

"Great!" I said. "Let's go before Dad finds somethin' for me to do." We hopped over the back fence and headed down the Henson fencerow.

16

These times were like heaven to me because I could actually enjoy the beauty of Mother Nature, which I found fascinating then, as well as now.

As we walked down the briery fencerow through some very thick grass, we could almost taste the air, it was so fresh after the rain. The spring wildflowers were just starting to pop up, and the mixture of yellow, purple, and orange flowers was breathtaking. We hadn't gone two steps until we almost stepped on a pair of bob white quail. "Look out, Bill," I kidded as the quail burst from cover. "That could have been a snake, so you better watch where you're walkin'."

Bill snapped, "Snakes don't scare me. Ain't no poisonous snakes around here anyway."

"Dad said we have some copperheads," I warned. Bill didn't have a comeback for that, but I noticed he started looking down more. "Why are we goin' over behind the Henson woods anyway? That pasture is on Mr. Vaughn's property, and you know how he is about crossin' fences."

"I saw some fox cubs out of their den in an old terrace a couple of days ago," Bill answered.

"Are you kiddin' me?" My heart started pounding so loudly I had to stop for breath.

"No, for real," he said. "I saw 'em!"

"Reds or grays?" I couldn't contain my excitement.

"I couldn't tell, but I did see two of 'em."

"Wonder why they were out of their den?" I asked. "I've seen lots of field dens in the spring but never any cubs."

"Can't figure it out either. I guess I've never seen any cubs out of their dens either."

"Maybe they're hungry," I suggested.

"Maybe the mother got shot or run over."

"Could be, but somethin' don't seem right. We'll know somethin's up if they're out again today."

I began running, not walking, toward the thick Henson woods, with Bill close behind. We made our way quietly through the thick woods to the southeast corner where we could get a better view of the terrace. Bill was telling me about it as we slowly peeked out of the fencerow and into the field. I couldn't believe my eyes. There they were, just like Bill said, two of the cutest, little furry fox cubs you could imagine. With the sun shining on their coats, they almost seemed to be wrapped in silk. We watched them for at least five minutes without speaking.

Neither one of us had ever seen anything like this.

"Bill, what do you figure? Why aren't they in their den, and where is the mother?"

"Got me, Cuz. The mother could be in the den or out huntin'."

The cubs didn't seem weak, but they weren't very playful either. It didn't look normal to me. We watched them for about 20 minutes, and they never did go into their den. Then I got the idea to try and find out if they had a mother.

"Bill, let's walk over and see if the mother's left any tracks since the rain, and if we don't find any, we'll smooth out all the trails with our hands and come back tomorrow to look for her tracks to see if she is comin' or goin'."

Bill said he reckoned that would work, so we hopped over the fence and moved cautiously toward the cubs. Of course, at the first sign of movement, they ran into the den faster than a ground squirrel. Bill and I looked all around the den for fresh tracks of the mother and found none. We brushed out a few old tracks with our hands and headed back home. The two cubs were all I could think about that evening as I finished my chores, had supper, and got ready for bed.

It was still too wet to plow the next day, so Bill showed up about the same time and we headed back to the old Hensen woods. Deep down inside, I was hoping that the cubs would not be there and that their mother had returned. But as it turned out, neither was the case.

Just like the day before, we eased our heads up over the fencerow, and there they were again. They were just as silky and beautiful as before but seemed a little less active than the day before. Today we didn't waste any time, just crossed the fence, and headed for the den.

Zoom! They hit the hole again just like before. We were somewhat puzzled by the fact that we found no sign of the mother's coming or going to the den. We decided to give it the rest of the day before any hasty decisions were made about taking these cubs if they were orphans. We left and came back around "dark-thirty." This time the cubs were not out, but as we approached the den we could hear them whining and crying from down deep inside the burrows. Again, we found no signs of tracks of the mother. Things were getting complicated.

As we walked back toward the house, I began thinking about trying to raise these guys on a bottle. I had some experience on this subject as I had raised a baby squirrel that fell out of its nest. "Squeaky" did real well, and I was even able to reintroduce him to outdoor life when he grew to be an adult squirrel. I kept thinking of Squeaky as we walked and recalled how hard it had been to feed him several times a day and keep him clean. I wondered if a baby fox would be harder to care for.

"Bill, do you think we can raise these guys if we have to?"

"I bet we can if we set our minds to it," he reckoned.

"It won't be easy; we'll have to hunt for them and everything."

"It might be fun though."

"What about your parents? What will they say?"

"They won't care," Bill laughed. "I'm always bringin' somethin' home."

"Mine will throw a fit. I'll have to try and convince Mom to soften the blow before I tell Dad." They both actually liked Squeaky after a while, but they seemed glad to see him go when I took him back to the pecan orchard to let him meet other squirrels. "Maybe it won't come to all of this. Maybe the mother will be there tomorrow, and we won't have to take them. I think I'll tell Mom tonight, just in case."

Later that evening, I asked my mother, "Mom, do you remember how Squeaky needed me and how we all saved his life?"

"Of course I do son, and you did a good job of raising him. But, as you found out with him, wild animals are meant to be in the wild."

"But aren't you glad we could help Squeaky, since he was an orphan and too young to take care of himself?"

She looked at me sort of puzzled, as to why I was bringing up Squeaky.

"What's up? Is there somethin' you need to tell me?"

"Well, not yet, but maybe tomorrow," I answered sheepishly.

"Now, Joe Ed, I hope you're not thinkin' of bringin' home another critter to raise."

I knew she was serious when she called me Joe Ed, so I answered cautiously, "I'm not sure yet, but it may have to be done, Mom. I can't just let them starve to death."

"Well, whatever you're plannin', you better clear it with your dad first because you know how he is about another mouth to feed around here."

"OK, Mom, if it comes to that, I will." I felt I had gone as far as I could go. They did like Squeaky and accepted him, so maybe they would do the same with the foxes, if it came to that. As far as Dad was concerned, I didn't dare ask him before the fact because he would definitely say no.

Luckily, the next morning there was so much dew that we still couldn't get back into the field to plow, so Bill and I went fox hunting again. There they were, just like before, but now they were whining and crying outside and wandering farther from the den opening. Bill and I looked at each other, and we both agreed we had no choice.

We jumped the fence, farther down the fencerow than usual, and worked our way in from behind the cubs. We crawled the last 25 yards on our bellies and through briers to keep from being seen. Then, at the last minute, we charged the two cubs. Bill covered the hole, and I scooped up one of the cubs. The other one ran back to the den, and Bill grabbed him. Our mission was accomplished. We looked one last time for any sign of tracks of the mother. Since we found none, we felt better about our decision as we started home.

Then reality hit us. What have we done? I looked at Bill, and Bill looked at me.

"Dad's gonna kill me," I rambled nervously.

"I don't know how to raise a fox," he blurted out.

We started running toward my home because there were no other options, in our opinion. We stopped at the last fencerow to catch our breath. As I looked down in my jacket pocket and saw those two brown eyes looking up from that jet-black face, it was love at first sight. I couldn't speak for Bill, but I decided right then and there that I would do whatever it took to raise this cub. Beyond that, nothing seemed to matter.

We got to the house and crossed the yard.

Dad hollered, "Son, where the heck have you been? I've been lookin' all over for you. You need to kill us a chicken for dinner and clean it. Then we have to fix that cultivator this afternoon. Looks like it's gonna be dry enough to plow by tomorrow. Where have you been?"

Although chicken for supper made my mouth water, I decided I might as well go ahead and "spill the beans." Keeping a pet fox from your folks would be pretty hard to do. I reached into my jacket pocket and pulled out the little gray ball of fur with its beady eyes, and to my surprise he had a white tip on his tail. He was a Red. I shoved it toward Dad and said, "Been huntin'."

"What in tarnation is that?" he yelled. "What have you done gone and brought home this time? It better not be a fox."

As he glared at me, I swallowed hard and said, "Well, uh, it is a fox, but he's an orphan."

"If he wasn't before, he dang shore is now," answered Dad. "Son, you just can't keep him. Foxes and chickens don't mix and you know that!"

"Yeah, Dad, I know. But I promise that as he gets older, I'll keep him tied, or on a leash, or with me. He won't kill our chickens." Last year, Dad had ordered a pure, registered line of Cornish game chickens from a hatchery up north, and they had just begun laying and producing chicks of their own. Not only was Dad very proud of his chickens, they were about our main food source.

"It'll never work," he said, as he stalked off toward his tractor, muttering to himself. "Chickens and foxes just don't mix. Anybody knows that."

I guess I took that as a definite "maybe," since I was running out of options, and set about locating a proper crate for my new companion. Bill took off home with his new buddy, and we both felt we were helping Mother Nature by adopting two of her orphans in need.

I found an old chicken crate, lined it with tow sacks, and placed the little cub in it. I put it in the corncrib and then started thinking about food and water. He was pretty small, so I figured he still needed milk. I found an old Dr Pepper bottle and mixed some fresh cow's milk with some water, about half and half, and then I put an old artificial ewe's rubber nipple on the bottle.

I headed toward the kitchen to find Mom to share the news with her. Besides, I was going to need her help to fix milk bottles and such. "Mom, look," I yelled as I ran into the kitchen. I pulled the baby fox from my pocket and pushed it toward her.

"Oh my, Joe, what have you done?"

"He doesn't have a mother," I quickly explained.

"And just how do you know that?"

I told her the entire story about our many trips to the den in hopes of her understanding the situation since she *was* a mother. All I got, instead, was a long silence and I hated that.

She finally said, "Well, you're on your own on this one. If you're old enough to decide to bring a fox home, you're old enough to raise it on your own."

"I'll raise him, I promise, and I won't bother you or Dad. Do you have a pan I can use to warm up this bottle?"

She reached into our cupboard and brought out a pan and handed it to me.

"Now what do I do?"

She turned on the stove and pointed toward the sink as if to say, "You figure it out."

I decided I had gotten all of the help I was going to get, so I set about warming the bottle myself. My first attempt at feeding was pretty messy, with me getting more milk on me than down the fox. Each day got better, though, as he learned to use the nipple and be a little slower and more patient as he nursed. In a few days, when he saw me coming, he would run and jump out of his crate and into my lap, with his little black ears held back and his tail and bottom wagging.

After a couple of weeks, it seemed that Mom and Dad weren't going to cause too much of a fuss, for the time being at least, so I decided to name him. Every time I looked at him or touched him, his fur was like satin or silk. I remembered the first time I saw him and how he looked so shiny and silky in the sun. It was only logical to call him Silky, and I later added his last name of Harris, for whatever reason I don't know.

So, lo and behold, Silky Harris was alive and well on the Cannon farm outside of Dublin, Texas. He thrived on his cow's milk and water and grew like a weed. I decided when he reached about 10 to 12 weeks of age to let him out of his crate for short romps with me and my border collie, Rintey (short for Rin-Tin-Tin). It was amazing how quick the three of us bonded. It was a good thing that Rintey and Silky got along so well because it gave Silky a much needed playmate and companion in my absence. I did have to keep Silky on a long lead line, but he had plenty of room to romp and play with Rintey when I was gone. I kept him beneath a large apricot tree down by the barn, and as he got older he began digging the most elaborate den system you can imagine. These holes not only occupied his mind, but also kept him cool in the summer and warm in the winter. Rintey was fairly small, so he would actually crawl down in the den to be with his buddy.

Best Pals — Silky and Rintey and myself on our daily romp.

As Silky Harris grew, his diet changed dramatically. I began feeding him rabbits that I would hunt for him when he was about four or five months old, and I started taking Silky with me on my hunts at about six months of age. I knew in the back of my mind that someday he would need to know how to hunt to survive on his own. This was a painful thought but a very realistic one.

On these training hunts, I left Rintey at home so Silky could concentrate on the business at hand: catching dinner. Silky and I would romp across the pasture and go down to the back fencerow, which was always good for a rabbit or two. It was during these hunts that I really began to get close to my companion, as well as develop a great respect for his speed and cunning. To have Silky running free beside me as we ran through the fields made me so happy. It seemed that when I was talking to him and playing with him, all my troubles and worries vanished. All I could do was marvel at his beauty and feel privileged that God had allowed me to be Silky's friend and share such wonderful times with him.

It was early December when we neared the fencerow during one of our routine hunts for his food. Silky was sporting his full winter coat, which was truly magnificent. By this time he weighed about 15 pounds and was quite a sight to behold. The tips on his ears and feet were coal black. The red in his coat was a bright reddish-orange with some occasional white and black hairs popping through. His white belly was brilliantly white, as was the distinguishing white tip on his tail. At first, his orange eyes had a mischievous look, but I began to notice that they seemed to be getting a serious look instead. I figured this was due to a combination of the hunting activity and maybe him reaching puberty.

Our first few hunts had turned out futile as we spent a lot of time finding, tracking, and then chasing the rabbits to no avail. We had some success on the next two hunts, where I introduced a new technique.

Since our tracking and chasing hadn't worked, I resorted to a more sly approach, which seemed to fit a fox. I simply taught Silky to "stay" and to "lie down." I did this by giving him rabbit hors d'oeuvres when he responded and did what I asked him to. Believe me, getting a hyper fox to "stay" was not easy, especially in the woods with rabbit trails running everywhere. Locating rabbits was never a problem around our farm. The rabbits thrived on our peanuts and the lush, coastal Bermuda grass that grew well in our sandy soil. With fencerows next to the fields and all the dense cover there, it was a rabbit haven. Being December, the trees had lost their leaves and even the green briers had turned brown. This color contrast made Silky stand out like a sore thumb, so I had to make sure he stayed as still as possible.

Early one Sunday morning I was trying to get a hunt in before church. As we went over the back fence, I caught my jacket on a brier and tore it a little. When I stopped to get it undone, I caught a glimpse of two deer moving out ahead of us. I took a couple of steps and heard a loud noise, which sounded like the flapping of wings. When I looked out over our neighbor's peanut field, hundreds of Pintail and Mallard ducks were bursting skyward from their nighttime roost in the open field. They stayed there at night to eat peanuts and sleep, and then flew away to surrounding lakes during the day. The sight of all this wildlife got my heart pounding, and I could only marvel as the cinnamon and white colors of the Pintails and the green and purple in the Mallards all mixed into a kind of rainbow effect. I watched until most of them were out of sight, but a few circled and drifted back in to continue their meal. It was time for me to get back to the business at hand.

I took Silky down the fencerow about 50 yards to the thickest part I could find and told him to stay and lie down. I hopped back over the fence and ran down below Silky about 100 yards. I started working my way back toward my companion, and I could see all of the cottontails breaking out of cover in front of me. They were running straight toward Silky.

I finally got back even with where I had left him and hopped back over the fence to look for him. He was not where I left him, which should have been a good sign. At least he had had something to chase. I looked and looked for him, but to no avail. At last I caught a glimpse of something red about 100 yards out in the peanut field and figured he had a long chase for a rabbit.

As I got closer, I knew that it wasn't a rabbit. It had feathers. Silky apparently got bored while waiting for me to flush out a rabbit and went off on his own quest. He had managed to sneak through the tall grass to a flock of those ducks and had caught one of them.

I was in awe and exclaimed, "I guess you don't need me, guy. Looks like you could even teach me a thing or two about huntin'. I know I couldn't have sneaked up on wild ducks. Of course, I'm not a fox, either." He paid no attention to me and just kept enjoying his duck breakfast. I was so proud of him and relieved to know that he could take care of himself if that day ever came.

Time passed, and winter turned into spring and spring into summer. Silky and I became more and more dependent on each other. He had won Mom and Dad over, and they actually played with him at times. On one particular sunny day, Mom and I had planned a fishing trip over to one of the Kiker tanks. I asked her if Silky could come along and was shocked when she agreed. Mom was the one who took me fishing since Dad was always working. She really liked to fish and could sit for hours and watch a cork, even if she didn't catch anything. She taught me how to have patience while catching fish and even showed me how to clean the fish when we were through. The two of us were pretty good at it.

I kept Silky on a leash for this trip since I didn't want anything major to go wrong. As long as he was on the leash, he did very well, but if I released him he would be off to the races.

We had been fishing for a couple of hours and had only caught a couple of little ones, so we were getting ready to go home. Then it happened. I got my line caught about two feet from shore, and Mom asked me what was wrong. "Hung up on somethin', I guess."

"Jerk on it and maybe it'll come loose," she said.

I gave it several tugs, but it didn't budge. Since it was so close to the bank, I decided to wade out and get it loose. I took one step into the water and did I ever get a surprise. My line took off and my little Sears & Roebuck rod nearly broke. When that rod bent double, it really got our attention.

I began floundering around in the water trying to hold that fish and yelling, "I'm goin' to lose him. Help me, Mom, help me!"

Mom couldn't swim so she wasn't about to jump in. When the struggle seemed futile, the fish made another pass close to the bank, and it was Silky that came to the rescue. That fox must have sensed that we were in trouble. He jumped into the water and grabbed that fish before we knew what was happening. He couldn't drag it, so he just put his paws on it and held it down.

I couldn't believe it — a fishing fox!

This seemed to stun the fish long enough for me to get a finger in his mouth and through his gills, and jerk him out on the bank. Silky was right behind me, jumping and biting at that fish with every step. He didn't know what it was, but he sure knew that he wanted it for himself.

Mom was in shock. "That is the most amazing thing I've ever seen," she said in astonishment. As we walked back to the pickup I could tell that Mom, for the time being anyway, had decided that Silky might be OK.

Since the fishing incident, I had begun to think to myself that I would have this fox forever, but things started taking a turn for the worst.

First of all, the apricot tree was Silky's home, and for the first time since Dad could remember, it did not bear any fruit. It really didn't appear to me to be dying, but Dad thought differently.

"You're going to have to get rid of that fox or move it," he informed me one morning on the way to the field.

"Why?" I asked with a puzzled look on my face.

"Because that apricot tree is dying. That fox of yours has dug so many holes around it until it has damaged the root system. I've seen it happen before. When a tree quits bearing fruit and starts to turn brown like that one is doin', it's as good as dead."

My heart sunk, and I got a big lump in my throat at the very thought of getting rid of Silky. I didn't answer Dad because I knew how he was when his mind was made up, and a 12-year-old boy sure wasn't going to change it. I just sort of tuned in on the "moving" idea and tuned out the "getting rid of" part of what he said.

The next day I simply relocated Silky to a large oak tree farther behind the house and thought the crisis was over. The apricot tree did go ahead and die during the next few months, and Dad made me chop it down and cut it into firewood as a subtle reminder as to whose fault he thought it was that we would no longer have any homemade apricot fried pies. To tell you the truth, I missed those, too. Mom sure knew how to make fried pies, and the fact that apricots were her favorite fruit didn't make her any more forgiving of Silky either.

It was along in October, and fall was definitely back in the air. The leaves were turning, and Silky had made himself several new dens as he prepared for winter. Everything seemed so rosy, and I should have known things were going too smoothly. I had been gone one afternoon on a very rare fishing trip with my cousin, and I was just heading through the front gate when I sensed that something was terribly wrong.

The first thing that caught my eye when I entered the yard was a huge pile of chicken feathers at the edge of the shrubs that surrounded our house. I just froze, not knowing what was going to happen next. My question was answered soon when Silky came around the house to greet me with a large Cornish game hen in his mouth and his collar missing. He was free and was definitely doing what foxes do — eating chickens. He couldn't have been any prouder of his prize and couldn't wait to show me his catch. He pranced around the house with that chicken in his mouth and wasn't about to let me catch him. I knew this was the end if Dad found out, and my only hope was to clean up everything before he saw it.

This idea was quickly squelched when out of the corner of my eye I saw Dad coming. Evidently, both Dad and I had happened onto Silky's victim at about the same time, and both of us had completely different ideas as to how to solve the problem. Dad ran by me and headed into the house without saying a word.

"Where are you goin'?" I cried as I chased behind him.

"You know where I'm goin'!" he yelled. "I'm gettin' my gun and endin' this problem right now. I told you that foxes and chickens don't mix, and you wouldn't listen. I told you to get rid of him, and you wouldn't listen. Now it's up to me to take care of it, and that's what I'm doin', taking care of the problem."

I grabbed his waist and, through the tears, managed to get out a few pleas of "Please, Dad, no! Don't kill Silky! Please, Dad, don't kill Silky!" I could see this wasn't working, and time was short so I headed for Silky. By then he was holed up in the hedges by the house and eating his prize. I crawled into the hedges and grabbed him by the scruff of his neck and headed toward the barn. I had no idea what this was going to accomplish, but I had to do something.

Dad came out on the porch and yelled, "Joe, stop, right now!" I froze in my tracks and waited. Dad soon appeared with his shotgun lying across his arm. "Put the fox down and go in the house," he demanded.

"No," I cried hysterically. "If I do, you'll shoot him."

Dad ordered, "Do as I said. I'm not goin' to tell you again. There's not but one thing to do to a chicken-eatin' fox and that's shoot him."

Hearing all of the commotion, Mom came running out on the porch and, to my surprise, joined in on the plea not to kill the fox. "Now, Bryce, you know how much that fox means to him, and it's not right to just kill him. He was only doin' what was natural for a fox. We have lots of chickens, and we won't miss one or two."

He came back with, "Adelle, you know as well as I do, the problem is not just that he has eaten two chickens. The problem is that now he's a chicken-eatin' fox and he won't stop."

Sensing that Dad was weakening a little, I started begging again, "Dad, if you won't shoot him, I'll get rid of him myself. I promise!"

I guess the sad scene of a crying boy holding his pet fox in his arms, refusing to let him go, and my mother being on my side, reached some sympathetic spot inside him. He actually started to cool off and even began to talk to me in a more rational tone. "Son, I know you love this fox, but he's still a fox and he can't survive in the wild and you can't keep him here."

"Dad, he can survive in the woods. I know he can! I'll take him off right now. Just please don't kill him!"

Dad looked at me with skeptical eyes, but he hadn't been on some of Silky's hunts and had no idea how he could hunt on his own.

Before Dad could revert back to his original idea of shooting Silky, I ran for our old 1941 Ford Pickup that Dad let me drive occasionally. "I'm takin' him right now," I said through the tears. "I'll be back later."

Since Dad made no active attempt to stop me or to drag me out of the truck, I took advantage of the momentary pause in the action and fired up that old pickup and drove down the road. I was still crying so hard I could barely see, and I had no idea where I was going or what I was going to do with Silky Harris. He just lay in the seat beside me and was looking up at me with chicken feathers still in his mouth, wondering why his picnic had been interrupted.

I took a right turn on our dirt road and headed north. It felt like my mind was spinning out of control as I drove up that country road. I didn't know where to take him, but I knew I couldn't take him back home. I remember telling myself, *Stop an' think! Just slow down an' think.* There was no answer to this. When I tried to slow down and think, all I could think about were the good times we had and how all that was over. He was my best friend, and I told him everything. Who could I talk to now?

As I drove and took deep breaths, I slowly started to feel a calmness coming over me. It was a relief in that I knew this day was coming and that because it was finally here, I didn't have to dread it any longer. Silky was not dead, and at least I had taught him how to survive out in the wild. I relaxed some and set out to find Silky a home.

I knew he needed to be far away from people to remove the temptation of coming up to them. If far enough away from people, he might even meet a female fox and become a dad, I told myself. I drove about 10 miles, back into an area where the road dead-ended into about a thousand acres of thick brush and timber. This big ranch had all sorts of wild game and varmints on it, as I remembered from hunting deer there the previous year.

I stopped the truck, cut off the motor, sat there for a minute or two, and then grabbed Silky and began one of the hardest walks I would ever have to make in my entire life. I would walk for a while, run for a while, and cry for a while. It seemed I must have walked for two or three miles back into those woods before I found a nice green area with a spring-fed creek nearby.

Silky had no idea what was about to happen, and he probably thought we were on one of our many hunts. It was then, and only then, that it hit me how to handle this. I would simply make him "stay" and say "down," just like when we were hunting. That way, he would not follow me. And when he became bored he would start hunting on his own, just like the day he caught the duck.

I found a big log, placed Silky behind it, and gave the commands to "stay" and "down." All I could do then was run as fast as I could toward the truck. And run I did. I never looked back. As the wind and branches hit me in the face, all I could think of was our great times together and how happy Silky would be now that he was free to hunt, be a daddy, and to run and play with other foxes.

That was the last time I saw Silky.

Bill's fox turned out to be a female, and he kept her for several more years. As she got older and more independent, she would run farther from home and would, on occasion, bring back her kill to the house. Bill tried to encourage her to hunt alone and figured that one day she would just disappear and go out on her own. That was exactly what she did. Bill saw a couple of foxes about two miles from his house while out hunting one day and thought that one of them was her, but she just turned and ran away. Bill said it made him feel good that, if it was her, she had found a mate and would be happy.

As I became a teenager and looked back on those days with Silky, I wasn't sure who taught whom. I really think I learned more from him about Mother Nature and about growing up in general. I learned how to be more nurturing, understanding, patient, and caring. All of these traits I would use later on in life while working with animals.

Silky had a lot to do with my decision to become a veterinarian, and more specifically to become an exotic animal veterinarian. The hands-on rearing of this fox made me very aware of the fact that wild animals have needs, desires, feelings, and sicknesses just like other animals. The wild factor often covers these things up, but they are there if someone will just take the time to understand them and care.

For bringing this respect, admiration, and understanding of wild animals out in me, I will always be grateful to Silky Harris and will never forget him as long as I live.

CHAPTER 2

BUCK AND KIWI

As I reached my teenage years, not a lot had changed in my life. The work on the farm was constant and seemed to increase as I got older, or so I thought. As the years passed, I became increasingly certain of my desire to become a veterinarian. Dad seemed to pick up on that and would always put me in charge of most of the veterinary related jobs.

These jobs included such things as helping ewes and cows with lambing or calving problems; vaccinating all of our livestock; dehorning cattle; and castrating pigs, lambs, and calves. Helping ewes with lambing problems became my specialty since my hands were small and I was able to manipulate the lamb into a position from which it could be delivered. I took a lot of pride in my sheep and with the loss of Silky I had used them to occupy my free time. I began raising purebred, registered Suffolk sheep to show and for profit. I had accumulated a fine herd that I had paid for with money I earned from my peanut crop. I had 20 head (19 ewes and one ram) and had a lot of blue ribbons to show for my entries at the local county fairs. My mom enjoyed the sheep and would take me to the shows with my sheep tied in the back of our truck.

All of my sheep had been looking good and doing real well on the show circuit. I noticed three or four, however, that seemed to be getting thin and losing their wool in spots. Since the rest of my flock was doing well, I just assumed it was due to parasites and de-wormed them again, using an extra dosage. It was in the summertime when sheep shed their coats, to some degree anyway, so I was not

My two prize Suffolk sheep.

too concerned. Then Dad asked, "Son, why are those sheep scratchin' all of the time? They're leaving wool all over the fences where they've been scratchin'."

"Just the heat, I reckon. I gave them an extra dose of worm medicine last week," I added.

"Well, you need to clean the wool off of the fences," he continued. Dad was a perfectionist, so I knew this simply couldn't continue. I started watching them closer and sure enough those three or four seemed to be constantly scratching their backs on the barbed wire fence. Each time they did, a large clump of wool would be left behind. I noticed they also were biting at their own skin and pulling out clumps of their wool with their mouths.

It was time to call for help, so we called our local veterinarian in Dublin, and he came out the next day. After examining the sheep, he pushed his hat back on his head and said, "Son, I don't recollect seeing anything like this in my 30 years of practice. It isn't mange and it's not an infection. I just don't know what the heck it is. I can tell you what I'm goin' to do. I'm goin' to call a federal veterinarian I know and tell him the symptoms and see what he suggests."

That sounded good to me, but several days passed before Scotty (short for Dr. Scott) came back.

I went running to his car and asked him, "What do my sheep have?"

"Well, Joe, we're still not sure. The federal veterinarian is comin' out himself to take a look. He thinks it could be a couple of things, and they may be reportable."

"Reportable? What does that mean?"

"Well, sometimes, if a disease is highly contagious to other animals and it's somethin' that can spread, then it must be reported to the federal authorities," he explained. "But don't worry, I doubt if it's one of those diseases because they're very rare."

I tried to put it out of my mind and went on with my chores, but in the back of my head, I knew Scotty was worried by the look on his face as he drove away.

About a week passed before two veterinarians drove up in a white car with a symbol of Texas on the door. They were very nice and asked if we could "lot" the sheep and help them get some skin and wool samples for testing. Dad and I were eager to help so we could get to the bottom of this. They seemed worried as they took wool, skin, and blood samples from the four ewes that were the worst, and five or six sheep at random with scruffy coats. I also noticed that Buck, my prize show ram, was starting to lose patches of wool. I was getting worried. As I pressed for an answer, I got the same old story, "We'll get back with you, but I doubt it's anything to worry about."

I was worried. I asked Dad, "What will they do? Why are all of these official-lookin' people comin' here?"

Dad answered, "Well, I don't rightly know, Son, but it's not ever good when the government gets involved. Quite frankly, I'm startin' to get worried."

The next few days seemed like forever as we waited for an answer. About 10 days had gone by when I noticed a different type and color of car coming up the road to our farm. It was sort of an army green color and it also had a symbol and writing on the door. As the car approached, I could feel butterflies in my stomach. I felt sick inside and I didn't know why. I knew an answer was coming and I was afraid I wasn't going to like it. A very tall and official looking man in a suit and tie got out of the car and introduced himself to us as Dr. Sheets with the United States Department of Agriculture.

"I am here to discuss your sheep," he began.

Dad pointed out, "They're my son's sheep."

Dr. Sheets looked at me and said, "Well, son, you and I need to have a talk."

I gulped and nodded.

He continued, "It seems your sheep have a very contagious disease called scrapie."

"What is that?" I asked.

"It's a disease caused by a virus that gets into the nervous system of the sheep and can eventually kill them," he explained. "The itching, scratching, and losing wool are only the early symptoms; furthermore, it's very contagious and will spread to all of your sheep."

"How does it spread?" As I asked, I felt the tears welling up in my eyes.

"Through the mouth from the saliva, and from eating with each other."

33

I looked at Dad for support or an answer in his eyes, only to find him standing there with his head down and his hands in his pockets. That was not a good sign. I still didn't understand what was happening so I asked the federal vet, "Can you give them some medicine for this scrapie?"

"There is no treatment, son. I am afraid it's fatal."

"Then what do we do? I don't want my sheep to die!" I could feel tears coming down my cheek.

"Joe, there's nothing we can do," he said. "I'm afraid your entire flock will have to be sent to slaughter."

"But they're my show sheep and all I have in the world!" I cried. "What about Buck and Kiwi, my two show sheep? We can't kill them, too!"

"I am sorry, son, but there's nothing we can do. We will pay you a fair slaughter price for them so you won't lose all of your money."

He didn't understand. It wasn't the money. Those sheep were my friends! They all had names and, after losing Silky, they had become my pastime. Now I was losing them, too. It didn't seem fair.

As I sobbed, the veterinarian explained that it was necessary to protect other sheep in other areas. The disease needed to be stopped before it traveled out of this flock, or even this county or state.

At this stage in my young life, I didn't understand what a virus was or how it could possibly cause an entire flock to be condemned to die. One thing I knew for sure: it must be a mighty powerful thing if there was no treatment except to kill them. This unknown virus that was killing my sheep awakened a great curiosity in me, and a strong desire to learn about the thing that had taken my entire flock of sheep.

CHAPTER 3

RED

It was spring again, my flock had long since been gone, and I had resorted to reading. There was nothing else around to occupy my spare time, and life without my animal friends seemed shallow. I wondered what the next few weeks would bring, but I knew that books couldn't hold my attention now with Mother Nature once again bringing newness to the all outdoors.

Strangely enough, however, it was a book that gave me an idea for my next animal adventure. You wouldn't have thought that *The Mongolian Hordes of Genghis Kahn* would provide any ideas to a teenager regarding animals, but in my case it sure did. I became captivated with the pictures and chapters about falconry. The idea of a bird of prey sitting on my arm and actually being trained to hunt was, for me, more than fascinating. I'm sure this was because I was missing that man-animal bond, which had become void in my life.

Falconry, as I discovered, was one of the most ancient forms of sport and hunting. During the days of Genghis Kahn, birds of prey were used for hunting food. It began to make perfect sense to me because I liked to hunt and liked all animals. Falconry seemed to be the answer for my next adventure. The main attraction to this ancient sport was definitely the strong bond that existed between the handler and the bird. I knew respect had to be earned and that would take time, but right then all I had was time.

Finding a proper falcon would not be an easy chore, especially since the best falcons were either duck hawks or peregrine falcons, neither of which were even found in the United States. Obviously, a substitute would have to be found, and that narrowed it down to two species of raptors that existed in North Central Texas: the red-shouldered hawk and the red-tailed hawk. In my immediate area, it was the red-shouldered hawk that was the most prevalent.

Well, I had decided on a species, so now what? How could I capture a hawk? Thinking back on my experience with Silky, I remembered how it had worked out great that I raised him from a baby. I decided on that same approach: catch a baby hawk. Ideas are easy, but in reality how could I find and raise a baby hawk? That was the mind-boggling question.

I was able to find a book about what young raptors eat, so all I lacked was the actual bird itself. It was late March, the leaves were coming out on the trees, the wildflowers were starting to bloom, and spring was definitely in the air once again. I had made numerous trips to the wooded area behind our house but to no avail. I had seen several pairs of hawks circling and hunting, but the trees in the woods were just too small for the hawks to build a nest in and raise their young.

I was getting frustrated when it dawned on me that I needed to expand my search and venture several miles from our farm. Since I had been driving the pickup on a more regular basis, this wasn't a big problem. I only needed to find the right time to slip off, but spring was the time that we did a lot of plowing to get the soil ready for planting. I would need to wait until we were caught up. Yet, if I stayed at home too long, Dad would definitely find something for me to do.

One Saturday afternoon, I told Dad I was going down on Greens Creek to do some fishing, grabbed my pole, and headed toward the old pickup. He simply nodded and said, "Stay out of trouble now, you hear?" I guess he sort of sensed that I was up to something.

I drove straight down the Dublin-Stephenville highway until it crossed Greens Creek, about three miles from our house. The area I was heading toward was Walker Lake, a fairly large soil conservation lake that dammed up Greens Creek some two miles farther down from where I would start walking. The more I walked and the closer I got to the lake, the larger and taller the trees were. It looked like hawk haven to me. The area was full of rabbits and field mice, and there was plenty of water. What more could a hawk want?

I saw two different pairs of hawks circling overhead, but no nests. I was about to give up when I looked up into a huge oak tree. There it was: an enormous nest made of large, dead sticks. This nest was almost in the top of the tree, and I could tell by the white stains on the edge of the nest that it had been used recently. This could be it!

The fact that I was deathly afraid of heights, however, was going to present a problem. I asked myself, How bad do you want this falcon? On the positive side, the wind was blowing lightly and the limbs leading up to the nest did look fairly large. To this day, I still don't know how I mustered up enough courage to try climbing it. I said to myself, *Here goes*, and off I went.

I started climbing, but I told myself not to look down at the ground. My heart was beating so loudly that the mother and father hawks could probably hear it from their lazy circles in the sky above. When I finally got to the nest, I was weak and tired from climbing and I was trembling all over from being so scared. At the same time, I was trying to hold on to a narrow, swaying limb with my legs, some 150 feet in the air.

What happened next was another event that helped me to understand the keen sense of survival that God has given to all of His creatures. Even now, as I look back on this day — as I have so many times during my career — I can only marvel at the intelligence of all species of animals and birds. As the limbs swayed and I finally got the nerve to stick my hand over the edge of the nest, I immediately had a greater problem than trying to hang on to that limb and cope with my phobia of heights.

Before I knew it, two sets of wings were beating me on the head, accompanied by a series of loud shrieks. Not only had both parents been watching me from the sky, they had waited until I got to the nest before beginning to protect their young. I could not believe what was happening to me and was reasonably sure I would be killed. If the irate hawks didn't peck or claw me to death, the fall would finish me off. Not knowing what else to do, I just froze and hung on tight to the tree limb with my legs.

After what seemed to me to be an eternity (but was probably no more than a few minutes), I was somewhat relieved that their dives were becoming less frequent. I seized the moment and thrust my hand into the nest one last time before heading back down the tree.

To my great surprise, I didn't feel feathers or little bodies, but several round objects. I didn't have a lot of time to think, and the hawks' screams were getting closer, so I carefully placed one of the eggs in my shirt pocket and slowly started backing down the limb. I decided that if I left at least two or three eggs in the nest, maybe they would not miss one, even though I had no idea what I was going to do with it.

I was never so glad to see the ground in my life but I was still shaking all over, partially from fright and partially from exhaustion. After I got my second wind, I ran across the open field to the pickup. I stopped now and then to look back at those beautiful birds, which were still circling close to the nest and trying to protect and guard their eggs. How wonderful Mother Nature is!

I drove back home and when I arrived it was getting close to suppertime. I knew I had to decide quickly what to do with my hawk egg because I knew it probably wouldn't last long if not kept at the proper temperature. In my head I was trying to figure out the old "light in the shoebox" trick when I walked into our old corncrib, and there before my eyes was the perfect solution.

Sitting on a bale of hay, almost perfectly camouflaged, was one of Dad's Cornish game hens. They were known to nest anywhere, and for some reason she had chosen the old crib and this particular bale of hay. If this worked it would be a lot more efficient than the shoebox — and a lot less trouble. When hens become broody and sit on a clutch of eggs, they are usually docile. I hoped this would be one. I carefully placed my hand beneath the hen to see what she would do. She never moved. With that, I slipped the egg under her and quietly shut the door to the crib.

Now all I had to do was wait the 21 to 28 days to see if the egg was fertile and would hatch. If it did, I would have a hawk. I wouldn't know what to do with it, but I would have a hawk.

I knew the hen only had just started sitting, so she wouldn't hatch anytime soon. Also, I had no idea what stage the hawk egg was in when I took it from the nest. Keeping all of this in mind, I checked the hen at least every other day. After two weeks, I was beginning to wonder if the egg was a dud.

On Day 16, I noticed the hen was acting strangely as I came into the crib. She was clucking and seemed nervous. I knew it was too early for her eggs to hatch, but I thought that maybe it wasn't too early for my hawk egg. Lo and behold, I lifted the hen up off of her egg and was greeted by the strangest looking creature I had ever seen. There, at the edge of the nest with a cracked egg around it, sat a ball of gray down with two huge, bulging eyes and a slightly curved beak. It was too tall and skinny to be a chicken.

As I sat the hen back down, she seemed almost as shocked as I was.

I guess there is no other way to describe the little creature than to say it was just downright ugly. Luckily, I had done some reading on the diet of young birds just in case my egg hatched, although I never dreamed it would.

I had an even greater problem than trying to feed it: I had to tell Dad that I had brought home another pet whose primary love in life would be to kill chickens and that one of his prize game chickens had hatched it. This was not going to be an easy task.

Dad had not forgotten the chicken incident with Silky, and he probably wasn't going to be very understanding about my bringing home Predator #2. Again, I had no choice. Hiding a pet hawk from my family would be impossible so I decided to take a different approach as I met him in the lot coming to feed the cows.

"Dad, somethin' strange is goin' on with that hen that has been sittin' on her eggs in the corncrib," I casually mentioned.

"What do you mean, Son?"

"Oh, I don't know, she's just actin' funny. She's cluckin' and seems nervous."

"She's probably hatched her chicks."

"No, it's too early. She's only been sittin' about 16 days. Why don't you check her?"

Dad went into the crib to do just that. I decided to follow since I really didn't know what he might do when he found this alien chicken. He watched her for a second or two when he opened the door, and by then there was movement beneath the hen's wings. "Yeah, she's startin' to hatch."

"You better check her," I persisted. "It's just too early."

He walked toward the hen and then observed, "See, she's hatched at least one already, but I've never seen a gray one or one with this much down on it."

As he looked at the little creature closer, he seemed to be in total disbelief. "Well, that's the most amazing thing I've ever seen. If I didn't know better, I'd say that this hen has crossed with a hawk or an owl, and I don't think that's possible."

As he looked over at me, he saw a sly grin on my face and then he asked me, "All right, what's up this time? What have you gone and done now? I'll declare, I can't let you out of my sight that you're not gettin' into somethin'. What in the world have you done?"

My grin had disappeared from my face as I related the story and my purpose to Dad. He just stood there in utter disbelief. I looked for some emotion in his face but saw nothing. He just stared right through me and said nothing for what seemed like an eternity.

Finally, he said in a relatively calm voice, "Son, I'm not goin' to argue with you about this. I know you went through a lot losin' your sheep and all, so if you are bound and determined to raise this hawk and train him to be a falcon — or whatever you call it — then you go right ahead. You know the rules though, one chicken gone and the hawk is gone."

With that, he walked out of the crib and never brought it up again. I really think the truth of the matter was that he never figured I could actually raise a hawk from an egg to an adult. As it turned out, I fooled him and myself because I really never thought I could either.

My food mixture for the baby hawk was pretty simple: gruel made of soybean meal, water, vitamins, and — what turned out to be my staple — boiled eggs. I fed it with an eyedropper and managed to get two or three droppers full down the hatch about four times a day.

The hen began to peck the hawk about two days later, so I moved it to a small chicken crate lined with burlap bags. I put a heat lamp over the crate to keep the temperature constant. The bird flourished, and before long some pinfeathers were starting to come in. One thing was for certain: he thought I was his mother and could actually recognize me. When he saw me walk into that crib, he would start opening his mouth and making a shrilled squeak.

The eyedropper quickly turned into a teaspoon and then a tablespoon as the young hawk grew to what I considered an enormous size. After 10 to 12 weeks he began to get his primary feathers and would sit on the edge of the crate and flap his wings. I took him outside once in awhile because the only exposure to sunlight he was getting was the light coming in through the barn doors. It was the bright color of his feathers and their red hue in the early morning sun that prompted me to name him Red.

I quickly learned that hawks, compared to foxes, have their own way of showing affection. When Red wanted me to scratch him behind his head, he would spread his wings, lower his head and make a subtle chirping sound. On occasion, when he was sitting on a fencepost or circling overhead, he would fly to me and try to land on my arm. If I didn't have my leather glove on, I found that this could be very painful, so I learned to wear it at all times when Red was loose. I also learned that hawks are very intelligent and almost calculating in their mannerisms, not to mention being much more quiet and patient than a fox. Red grew into a magnificent specimen with a beautiful mixture of white, brown, and light reddish feathers. As it turned out, Red was a red-shouldered hawk and not a red-tail. His parents would have been proud to see him full grown. I could only hope that I could teach him to hunt as well as they would have.

I started adding small rodents and lizards to his diet when he reached four months of age. By six months, his diet included rabbits almost exclusively. There was still an abundance of cottontails and jackrabbits around, and these rabbits could do serious damage to our peanut vines if left to thrive on their own so Dad sure didn't mind me taking a few for Red.

By this time Red had moved into a small chicken house with a screened-in area where I had built a perch for him. From there, I would take him out every day and allow him to sit on my arm, which was covered with a thick glove. I kept him tied to my wrist with a long, leather cord tied gently to his leg. He seemed to adapt well to the cord and never acted like he wanted to fly off. He would get excited when he saw a rabbit or a field mouse, and that was a good thing if he was going to become a good hunter. For the time being, we just took walking trips together and

Red at home in his house.

41

became close.

My first attempt at training him to hunt came in the backyard. I sat Red on top of a fencepost, with no ties, and tossed small bits of rabbits, his favorite food, up into the air. He sat there and screamed but couldn't figure out that I wanted him to catch them in midair. As the pieces hit the ground, he would fly down from his perch and grab them and eat. I finally made a dummy out of a sack, with feathers attached to it, in order to excite him. The feathers really got his attention.

After several weeks of watching me throw this dummy up in front of him, he finally got the picture and started flying up toward it. I rewarded him with rabbit morsels each time, and we started to really make progress. It had been a long process, but we were finally getting to that level of mutual respect and admiration that I had been seeking all along.

Red allowed me to show off his wing spread.

I truly loved and missed Silky, but I will have to admit that having this magnificent bird of prey sitting on my wrist — his whole purpose in life being to please his master — left me in total awe. It just seemed that after every experience with an animal, I wanted to learn more and more about them. I wanted to learn how animals think, and I wanted to help preserve God's beautiful creatures in any way I could.

Red and I never reached professional levels of falconry, probably because he was not a falcon. He never learned to circle and attack small birds in midair but was able to finally catch a dove or two. Because of his limitations, we mainly hunted small mice and rabbits. Red loved this game because every day he got to eat what he was hunting.

I kept Red for about two years before the inevitable happened. I knew that sooner or later he would have to be released, and I also knew that, like Silky, he could take care of himself when that day came. I wasn't worried about that.

The incident that nudged Red out into the real world came in basically the same manner. I had gone out to his cage to take him on his afternoon hunt when I noticed the door ajar. Either I hadn't fastened the latch or the wind had blown it open, and Red was not to be found. I searched and searched but to no avail.

It was beginning to get dark when I suddenly heard a flapping of wings. I turned around to see Red fly up from the hedgerow behind me. I was relieved in one breath and scared in the next: I wondered what he had been doing in that hedgerow for that length of time. It didn't take me long to figure it out as I leaned over and looked into the area where he had been sitting. One thing was for certain; I didn't need to feed him that night. When a young hawk eats a whole Cornish game rooster, he simply shouldn't be hungry.

I never told Dad about the rooster, and he never asked what happened to his prize rooster. Dad discovered that Red had disappeared shortly after the rooster was missing, so I think he figured it out.

I already knew what I would do with Red when it was time to return him to his world. I got back in the truck and traveled down the same road. This was becoming a habit, but this time I felt OK about it. For one thing, I was older and knew I had only borrowed him from Mother Nature for a short time. I would miss him; but, like Silky, he could find a mate, hunt for himself, and live his life to the fullest.

It was only appropriate to take him back to the very tree from which I had removed him as an egg. This was a beautiful place, lying along a creek and in an area full of game. It was the perfect place for him to experience his freedom. Since it was almost dark, I knew Red would be content to roost in that tree for the night and not try to follow me home. Of course, when I released him I did cry and I missed him terribly; but afterwards, whenever I would drive by that area and see hawks circling high in the sky, I felt warm inside and happy for Red because I was sure he was happy, too!

CHAPTER 4

EARLY DAYS AT THE WILDLIFE PARK

A lot happened during the next 10 years of my life. I was 24 years old and fortunate enough to achieve a goal that I had set years before: to be a veterinarian. In 1972, after years of education and training in Texas and California, I was on my way back to Texas to begin my first major job in exotic animal medicine. I certainly had mixed emotions as I drove down that road heading back to Grand Prairie, just 90 miles from where I was born and raised. On one hand , I would miss all of my friends, both animals and people. On the other hand, I couldn't wait to take the reins of my new position as resident veterinarian for the International Wildlife Park. This was a huge undertaking for me and a tremendous responsibility, since this park was billed to be the main holding facility for one of the largest collections of exotic animals in the world.

I felt much more confident than I had been two years earlier, but I still didn't feel totally comfortable about my exotic animal medicine skills. I probably would not have developed my exotic animal interests at all without Dr. Murray at UC Davis, who taught me two main things about exotics, which seemed to really whet my enthusiasm for treating them. First, he taught me some very subtle signs to watch for, which enabled me to tell early on if a wild animal was sick. This was extremely important because, if you couldn't detect illness in its early stages, you had little or no chance of helping an animal in the later stages when it was showing obvious signs of sickness.

The second important thing that Dr. Fowler taught me was chemical immobilization. This allowed me to use drugs to capture and immobilize even the wildest of animals, so that I could examine, draw blood, and treat any problem that they might have. We treated a lot of exotics at Davis, primarily at the Sacramento Zoo. Dr. Fowler cared for the zoo's animal collection and allowed the seniors in vet school or any interested interns to rotate through that area as desired. After I left Davis and moved to Southern California, I volunteered on weekends at Lion Country Safari in Laguna Hills, California. This provided me with basic hands-on

Animal capture and movement without the use of tranquilizers.

experience and a chance to work on animals that roamed in the open park, with its drive-through concept. Here I used a lot of chemical restraints and began to understand just how wild these animals were.

I will never forget one incident in which we were immobilizing zebras to trim their feet and draw blood. We were using a product called succinyl choline chloride, which temporarily paralyzes the muscles but does not render them unconscious at all.

I remember Pat Quinn, the director of the Laguna Hills Park, saying, "Joe, when you put the masks on those zebras or get around their mouths, be careful because they can still bite!"

Well, I didn't really understand how hard they could bite until I had a first-hand encounter immobilizing some Hartman zebras to collect blood for a Coggins test. Everything had gone by the book so far. The dart had hit one zebra square in the hip. He ran for about 40 or 50 yards, began to stagger, and then fell on his side as they always do.

A ranger was applying a halothane gas mask over the zebra's nose in order to keep him down longer if necessary, and I was beginning to draw the blood. The next thing I heard was a blood-curdling scream coming from the ranger. I turned my head a few inches to see the facemask on the anesthetic machine covered with blood. At first it didn't register with me until I looked at the ranger clutching his hand, which he had wrapped in

Public Relations photo taken at Lion Country Safari, Laguna Hills, California.

a towel. Then it hit me; the zebra had managed to bite off his fingers! As it turned out, only one finger was missing, and as bad as it was, it could have been much worse.

So, my first major lesson with exotics was to always respect them and never underestimate what they can do. Looking back now over the years, it seems that every time I didn't follow what I had learned that day and somehow got lax, the worst happened. The other thing I figured out was that there had to be a better drug out there for zebras than the succinyl choline chloride.

All of these thoughts and experiences kept running through my mind as I drove down the highway toward Grand Prairie. Everything I had experienced in California only served to better prepare me for what lay ahead in my new job. As I drove toward Texas, my mind also wandered back to the farm in Dublin and to the days with Silky and Red. It had become clear to me that I was meant to work with exotic animals all along, and this gave me a feeling of contentment.

The Wildlife Park was still in the final stages of construction, so this would give me some time to get my feet on the ground, meet management, and learn my way around before I became so involved in animal care that

I had no time for anything else. After getting my wife and newborn son settled in, I ventured out to the park for my first visit. I quickly discovered over the next few days and months that, no matter how well qualified I thought I was for this job, I had no clue about what lay ahead of me.

As I got out of the truck and made my way into the main office, I was promptly introduced to my new supervisor, Bill York. He was the man in charge of all of the animal operations for International, and would be in Texas until the park was completely up and running. Bill was a South African, and quite an imposing force with his red hair, broad shoulders, and thick South African accent. I actually had met Bill in passing at the Laguna Hills Park during my short tenure there, although I didn't think he would remember me.

"Joe, how in the bloody hell are ya? It's good to see ya."

"It's good to be here, Bill. I can't wait to get started."

"We've got plenty to start on," Bill began. "I thought they were never going to send me a vet. I've been having to do it all myself, and frankly I'm not doing it justice with all of the construction going on at the same time. Joe, let's get right to it. Here are the bloody problems as I see them. Basically, we have too many animals together in these smaller interim holding compounds. This causes fighting, and the stress from the conflict, plus being in smaller pens, leads to disease. It's been mainly upper respiratory and gut problems so far, but we haven't lost any yet. To further complicate things, they're sending us new animals every day, and basically we have nowhere to put them. We only have about 25 percent of our inventory on the grounds with only four months to go until the park opens in the spring. This picture gets even bleaker when you take into consideration that winter is coming on.

"Joe, in a nutshell, you're just going to have to bloody handle all the animals that are here and the new ones coming in. I'll give you my best ranger, Verne, and his crew to help you. Between the two of us, we'll get 'er done, eh?"

This wasn't quite the gradual introduction to the park I had expected, but, oh well, a good adventure is always fun. "Where do I start, Bill? What are the priorities for now?"

"Grab Verne and head to the compound. He will fill you in. I know we have a couple of newly arrived giraffe with pneumonia that will need

IVs. One wildebeest got gored yesterday and needs attention. All of the young elephants need vaccinating, as does the entire collection, for that matter.

"And by the way, the coyotes from the Trinity River are coming in at night and trying to drag down our smaller antelope. Sounds like Africa, huh Joe? We have to plug those holes in the fence, set traps, post a guard at night, or whatever it takes. We can't let the coyotes destroy our population. Oh yeah, one more thing, you will be going to New York to meet our rhino shipment when it arrives and accompany it from New York to Grand Prairie. By then, James Ashe will be here to help me out, and I hope to give you some relief, as well. Good luck, Joe! Ta-Ta!"

And I thought I was prepared! How could anyone be prepared for this? My only hope was that Verne would be able to give me some guidance on what to do.

The questions raced through my mind: how do I IV a giraffe, treat a gored wildebeest, establish a predator control program, and vaccinate the entire animal collection? Vaccinate them with what? I stormed from the main building to find Verne. I also had met Verne briefly in California and, unless things had changed, I didn't feel real good about Verne bringing a sense of calmness and organization to the situation.

I looked all over the maintenance and hospital areas for Verne but to no avail. I even went back to the office and tried to call him on the radio but couldn't get a rise there either. So I went ahead and drove out into the compounds alone, looking for him. I asked the guard at the front gate if Verne was out in the park.

"I reckon he's out in Section II. Be careful out there, Doc. He may have the cats out," he warned as he opened the gate.

As I drove through Section I, I could only marvel at how similar it looked to the pictures I had seen of the plains of Africa. They had built burms, planted trees, created lakes, and had done everything possible to make the animals feel at home. Toward the end of Section I was a second holding pen that was serving as a temporary home for the hoof stock. When Section I was complete, this pen would be torn down and the animals released into their new home. At first glance, all of the animals appeared happy, healthy, and content.

As I arrived at the Section II gate, the guard stopped me and wanted to know who I was and what I wanted.

"Just looking for Verne," I explained. I told him who I was and that I needed Verne's help to treat a couple of sick giraffe.

"Good luck," he laughed as he opened the gate into the lion section. "Verne's been kinda edgy lately. Be careful in there, Doc. He may have some cats out."

I assumed it must be Verne's job to get the cats trained to go in and out of their huts on command. After a few minutes of driving, I reckoned that was exactly what he was doing. Section II was almost like a jungle, with dense vegetation, numerous willows, thickets, trees, brush, and basically just a whole lot of places for cats to hide if they didn't want to be seen or didn't want to be penned up. The cats were turned loose to roam free in the section by day and housed by night. As one might correctly presume, this could be a nightmare for personnel and management. Nobody feels comfortable with the idea of working a pride of lions in a small, zebra-striped Jeep. Maybe that's why Verne was always on edge. To add to his jitters, he had been responsible for the cats at the wildlife park in California, as well, and had some close calls there before being transferred to Texas.

As I rounded a corner, I found myself at the dens used to house the lions at night. Verne's Jeep was parked there, but Verne was not in sight. The dens were full of lions, and I could only assume that all of the cats were enclosed.

I cautiously eased out of the truck and yelled for Verne. No answer. I yelled again, "Verne, where are you?" I noticed some movement in the grass beside my truck and expected to see Verne pop out at that point, but that's not exactly what happened.

Instead, a full-grown male lion simply stood up from the grass and began walking toward me. His glaring, reddish-orange eyes were fixed on me, and he was making a low, growling sound in his throat. I remember being amazed at how massive these cats appear up close. This looked to be a young male, maybe two or three years old, but even this guy weighed between 400 and 500 pounds. He was huge and definitely coming for me.

My heart was beating so loudly I was sure the lion could even hear it. I was getting so weak in my knees that I could hardly stand. In other words, I was horrified! I had no idea what to do and didn't know if I had time to get back in my truck so I did the worst possible thing next to running: I just froze!

The cat didn't seem vicious, but it was continuing to walk toward me. I truly felt I was history. About that time, I heard a loud pop and saw the lion whirl in a circle and growl loudly. With this, I exploded into my truck and slammed the door. By this time I could see a metal dart hanging from the lion's hip, and he was staggering somewhat.

As if from nowhere, Verne appeared from the bushes. "Take that!" he yelled at the cat as the lion began to circle and then lie down quietly on his side.

I was still too scared to move and was only able to stare in disbelief at the sleeping lion. I marveled at how close I had come to being his dinner and recording one of the shortest first days on the job in history.

"Welcome to Texas, Doc," laughed Verne. "You were never in danger. I was watching him all along, but I couldn't warn you because that might've ruined my shot. I've been trackin' and stalkin' that lion for two days. He wouldn't go up with the rest, and I just couldn't get a shot at him. I figured he would come back to the dens, so I baited him down here and fixed up a tree blind. It paid off. You can bet he won't go out anymore. He's just a loner, I guess. Doc, are you all right? You look a little pale. If the dart hadn't worked, this would have," he said as he held up his .44-Magnum pistol.

"Glad it didn't come to that," I gulped, still in disbelief.

"What can I do for you?"

"I forgot." I smiled faintly as I felt the blood rushing back to my face. "Oh yeah, I remember. Bill York told me to find you and get you to help me treat two sick giraffe, figure out a vaccination and de-worming program for every animal, plus discuss predator control."

"Well, I'd like to help you, but the best I can do is to assign you a ranger to help, so you're basically on your own. It's not that I don't care, Doc, but I just don't have time. They've got me covered up. I've got 30 lions to break to these huts, and as you see that's not by any means goin' perfect. In Section III over there, they want me to run 30 adult cheetahs free with hippos, rhinos, and Cape buffalo. And the cheetahs have to go in and out daily just like these lions. I'm not even sure the cheetahs won't eat the Cape buffalo, but the bosses tell me they won't, so I guess I'll go ahead and organize it anyway.

"So, basically, you're in charge of the sick giraffe, the vaccinations, and the predator control; but I'll give you one man to help you. Get on the radio and round up John Clay. He's my senior ranger and he can ride with you and help. If you need me, try my radio or I'll be in Section II or III breaking in cats."

"John Clay, come in," I desperately pleaded on the radio. I had a feeling I was getting the runaround, but it seemed everyone's plate was just full. John answered and at least sounded helpful on the radio. After meeting John and talking with him, I found him very willing to help, but there was just one problem: John was more inexperienced than I was. He had never worked with exotic animals at all, only with farm animals. But he knew the basics, was sure willing to help, and had been there long enough to know his way around. At least he knew where the giraffe were.

After finding and examining them, I found it was obvious that they didn't feel well. This wasn't good because I knew that if a wild animal was sick enough to clinically show it, then it was near death. Both of the giraffe seemed sluggish and had their necks distended in an effort to breathe properly. They were even making a gurgling noise when they tried to inhale and exhale.

"Full blown pneumonia, John," I said. "These guys are plenty sick."

"What do we do, Doc?"

"Well, they need IV antibiotics or they'll die."

"How do we do that?"

"Well, I'm relyin' on you, John. You're the experienced one here."

"If it was a cow, we would just squeeze her up and treat her, but I don't know how these things will take to squeezin' or even to a needle." John, of course, was referring to the days on the farm when he used to work cattle through a large, metal squeeze chute. The animals were driven through a chute where their head was caught and then their body squeezed, or confined, to keep them reasonably still. Unfortunately, we didn't happen to have a squeeze chute available.

"Well, they have to be treated, so let's just do it. If you'll get me somethin' to stand on we'll see how they'll react to a needle."

John found me a couple of bales of hay, which at least put me at shoulder level so I could reach the jugular vein. I had never been this close to one of these beautiful animals, and my heart was fluttering with excitement. Or I guess it could have been a flutter left over from the lion episode.

The beauty of these majestic animals began to occupy my mind and allowed me to forget about the lion. Their long eyelashes and soft, pliable noses were the first things to really hold my attention; then, as I gazed down the neck, I couldn't believe its length, size and texture. Each cervical vertebra must have been one-and-a-half feet long, and the skin itself was very thick and leathery. I couldn't help but notice the circular, brownish, cream-color pattern of this reticulated species of giraffe. The way the colors blended throughout the body looked like they were designed and painted by an artist. In a way, they didn't look real.

I was so enthralled with the beauty of this animal that I found it hard to concentrate on my treatment. When I inserted the needle into the jugular vein, the giraffe just stood there. I was amazed, but again these were very sick animals. Both giraffe allowed us to give the IVs with only a minimal struggle. By the fourth or fifth day of injections, they did require more squeezing, which we were able to do with more bales of hay. The injections proved to be life saving for our new giraffe friends. They both lived and did well.

With the successful treatment of giraffe behind us, John and I began thinking about vaccination of the hoof stock and predator control. The vaccination of the hoof stock was a long and laborious task since they had to be done individually with the use of a Palmer Capchur dart. This involved putting the vaccine, usually 5 to 7 cc, in the metal cylinder and then twisting the needle on one end and the tailpiece on the other. The needles we used were colored and would hit the animal, then bounce or fall out. Getting a good, clear shot became harder since the animals quickly figured out what was going on and recognized my vet truck. I had to resort to riding out with the feed trucks and in different Jeeps to disguise what I was doing. We finally managed to get the job done. After a month, we had vaccinated some two hundred head of hoof stock and rid the park of about 20 coyotes.

I never ceased to be amazed by the beauty and magnificence of all of the African exotics. We had wildebeest, lechewee, kudu, water buffalo, Ankoli cattle, zebra, eland, Biesa oryx, Scimitar horn oryx, Sable antelope, and Sitatunga, just to mention a few. Having accomplished our goals for the first month, John and I moved on to bigger and better things. Little did I know that the next phase of my job would almost cost me my life.

Giving an IV to a giraffe with pneumonia while Fred Coston and a ranger (left) observe.

A family of Nilgai in Section I holding pen during the early days at the park.

White Bearded Gnu (Wildebeest) in Section I holding pen during the early days at the Grand Prairie, Texas park.

CHAPTER 5

DAMIEN AND THE CAPE

I was actually beginning to feel comfortable around these wild creatures and almost even lucky. Since my brush with the lion, things had been pretty anti-climatic and routine. I had a gut feeling that was about to change. When you get comfortable, you get careless. You can never underestimate the intelligence of God's creatures.

John and I had vaccinated everything in Section I without much excitement, so we decided to move into Section III, which turned out to be a little tougher. At that time, it was home to the young African elephants and 10 head of Cape buffalo. The elephants had been recently imported from a game preserve in South Africa, where they had been orphaned due to poachers. It was hoped that they would thrive in this controlled environment and eventually become reproducing adults. The hippos, rhinos, and chimps had not been delivered yet, and the cheetahs

Unloading new arrivals of African elephants.

were kept enclosed at night, so we figured we would vaccinate the cats in their huts.

The group of elephants we had received from South Africa included mostly orphans. Their mothers either had been killed by poachers or had died as a result of disease or starvation. The South African government did not have enough facilities to house these orphans, and this was where International Animal Exchange became involved.

The elephants were housed in a cinder-block house about 150 feet by 150 feet in size. Since they were young and not really old enough to be trained, they were simply coaxed in and out as a group by the placement of feed, and this seemed to work fairly well. I actually handled and rubbed several of the tamer ones on occasion and I really didn't consider them to be wild at all. The largest elephant in the group was approximately four to five feet at the shoulder and weighed about 800 pounds. Their trunks were only about 3 to 3-1/2 feet long. Overall, they were fractious, but seemed relatively harmless. I had heard how smart elephants were and, being herd animals, how they protected each other, but it's hard to know what intelligent, wild animals are thinking.

It was early one fall morning when John and I drove up to the elephant house equipped with some 30-odd syringes of tetanus and sleeping sickness vaccine that we planned, somehow, to get into these pachyderms.

"Well, what do you think?" I asked. "How do we handle these guys?"

John responded with his usual, "Well, if they were cows, we would squeeze them and just stick 'em."

"Works for me. Since they're pretty crowded in their house, let's just walk around 'em an' stick 'em when we crowd them into a corner, an' then mark 'em with this yellow marker. I think I can stick 'em before they know it and react."

So John and I walked into a closed-in room and began sticking 15 fractious African elephants with our vaccine. These elephants were captured wild and hindsight told me that I should have taken this into consideration. I remember the air being unusually clean and fresh that morning, as all of my senses were literally inflamed. The excitement of being around and getting my hands on wild African elephants made my heart race.

John and I stopped outside of the barn and surveyed our patients. I was amazed at how quickly they could move and abruptly spin in another direction. The larger ones would wheel, flare their ears, raise their trunks in alarm, and then turn and go about their business. They even would kick out in all directions with their rear legs, occasionally hitting one of their buddies with a glancing blow, as if to serve a warning not to get too close.

African elephants at home in the park.

All of this seemed to me to be what young African elephants do, so it appeared to me they were harmless. My last thought before going inside was how privileged I was to be handling African elephants in Grand Prairie, Texas.

As we methodically moved among the excited pachyderms while giving them their inoculations, it was almost too easy. John held my tray, and I injected the elephants one at a time in the back leg and then marked them with a yellow marker. The elephants would jump or whirl, some would even trumpet, but overall it was going well.

By the time we had gone through 10 or 12 of the 15, I had totally lost all fear of anything bad happening and I was not watching my patients nearly as close as I was when I first started. Since then I've had plenty

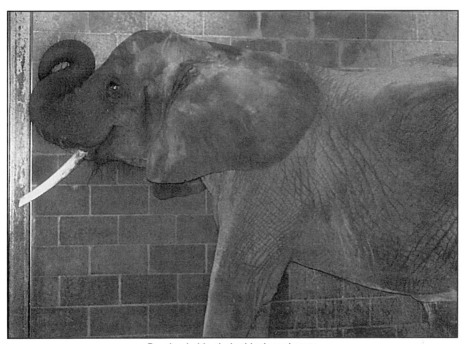

Damien in his cinder block enclosure.

of time to ruminate what happened next with a young elephant by the name of Damien.

The amazing thing to me was that Damien was not an animal that I was vaccinating or one that I had already vaccinated. He was one that I hadn't done yet, but he had obviously been watching me and apparently didn't like what I had been doing to his friends. To this day, I think that he watched, waited, planned, and then grabbed me when my back was turned to take full advantage of the element of surprise.

I was almost through — only one or two head away from complete success — when I felt an elephant trunk wrap around my waist. I squirmed and managed to turn around but couldn't break the grip; it was like a python's death grip and it was coming from the largest of the young elephants, Damien. He was the leader of the young band and obviously the protector, as well.

As I faced my captor, I was eye to eye with Damien, and he was fighting mad. You could actually see the anger in his eyes. To this day I am certain that, if he had known how to kill me instantly, he would have.

Being young and not sure how to deal a deathblow, he settled for violent thrusts back and forth, up and down, and around, instead of slinging me to the ground and pounding my chest or skull with a foot. He kept his trunk tight at all times. It was around my chest and not my arms, but it might as well have been around them, too, as I found them totally useless.

When you are being slowly asphyxiated due to an inability to expand your chest at all, nothing works, including your brain. You are aware of what is happening but helpless to do anything about it, and everything seems to be in slow motion.

Although parts of the incident are still a blur in my memory, parts are still crystal clear. One thing that still burns in my mind is that when Damien got tired of slinging me around like a rag doll, he decided to just press me up against the cold, cinder-block wall and steadily push. With the top of his head in my chest, Damien seemed content to plant his rear feet and try to push me through the wall, using an occasional head rotation for added pressure. He was going to make sure that I never harmed his friends again, and he was doing a good job!

I could literally feel my ribs start to separate from my sternum and was just about ready to pass out when I heard voices yelling and screaming, and then felt Damien's grip lessening on my chest. As Damien turned to face his new enemies, I hit the floor with a thud.

The next thing I remember was John and two of his rangers dragging me outside. Things were still blurry, and I remember trying to breathe as I lay on the ground. My chest felt like an elephant was standing on it. As I desperately tried to inhale and get oxygen, the pain became so intense that I passed out. The next thing I remember was waking up in Arlington Memorial Hospital and still feeling like an elephant was on top of me. The pain had not gone away, but a machine helped me breathe so I could at least get oxygen and stay awake.

Luckily, I survived with only four broken ribs. Everything healed well, and within 30 days I could hardly tell that anything ever happened. God was with me that day and allowed me to live to experience many more lessons in animal behavior.

I was able to make my daily rounds at the park over the course of the next month but refrained from any rigorous activity for as long as I could.

I still had not completed my vaccination program in Section III and was determined to do that before going on to other things.

We were able to vaccinate the cheetahs in their huts since they were put up at night, and all we lacked were the Cape buffalo. I thought about it long and hard, and I couldn't imagine what could go wrong if I used a Capchur rifle to vaccinate the Capes, which were free to roam within the 20-acre section. Not only could I be standing a good distance away from them, but I would also have plenty of room to escape to safety if anything went wrong.

I had drawn up all of my vaccine and was ready to start the following morning when Bill York called me to come to the office.

"Joe, the reason I called you in was to tell you that we need to capture two of the younger Cape buffalo out of Section III for shipment to our Ohio park."

Well, I hadn't done any immobilizations on my own at that time, so it kind of caught me off guard. "Uh, sure. When do you need them to be caught?"

"Tomorrow if possible. They need to be in Ohio by the weekend for an overseas shipment that is leaving from there. I know you haven't done too many of these immobilizations, but I will give you my new senior ranger to assist you and however many of his crew that you think you need. His name is Ron Surratt, and he will be splitting the senior ranger duties with John Clay. I'm going to put John and Verne in charge of the cats, and Ronnie will oversee hoof stock."

"OK, Bill, whatever you say. We'll handle it. I was goin' to vaccinate the Capes anyway tomorrow, so I'll just do it all at once."

I walked from the office. *This is just great. Not only am I doin' a new procedure tomorrow, I'm doin' it with someone I don't even know.* At least, according to Bill, Ron had some experience working with exotics.

"Ron Surratt, come in please!" I pleaded on the radio. I had hoped to meet him today and get a plan of action for tomorrow.

"Go ahead, this is Ron," he replied.

"This is Dr. Cannon. Can we meet and talk about our new assignment?"

"Sure, I'm at the nursery. Come on down."

Ron had been hired recently, and although I had heard about him

I had not officially met him. He had been a senior ranger at the Ohio wildlife park for several years and had a great deal of hands-on animal experience.

As I walked into the nursery, I was met at the door by a very calm and laid-back person.

"I hear we have some Capes to catch tomorrow," Ron noted, as we shook hands.

"That's right, an' I don't know about you, but that's a new one on me."

"Me, too!" he smiled.

"Oh, great, here we go again." I laughed. Ron didn't seem too worried about our new assignment, and this gave me a great deal of confidence, knowing I would be working with someone who had experience.

"Do you have any M-99?" Ron asked.

"As a matter of fact, I do. I haven't used it on Capes before, but M-99 I have."

"If you'll get the 99 and the capture equipment, I'll meet you out there early in the morning and we'll get started. Doc, I also can tell you one more thing about Cape buffalo: they can be mean as can be and they're very territorial." Ron walked out the door, with me following.

"Maybe they haven't been in the section long enough to become territorial," I added as I walked off.

The next morning turned out to be the morning of our first frost, and it was plenty cold as Ron and I hooked up the red horse trailer to his pickup.

"A good morning for huntin' Capes, Ron."

"Joe, these things are so unpredictable that I'm not sure any morning is a good morning to hunt Capes. Actually, it's not the hunting that's the problem, it's the capture and generally working with them after you find them," he chuckled.

"How do you plan to load these two Capes after we catch them?"

"Very carefully," he joked. "I thought that since the two that we're going to catch are younger animals — about 800-pound yearlings — we could load them in this red trailer. How we get them in there is up to you and the drugs."

"Maybe I can give them a walkin' dose, an' we can basically lead them in."

"That'll work! The less we have to drag these things, the better. Joe, I figure after they're up and out from under the drug, we can transfer them to a crate for hauling to Ohio."

It seemed to me that we were devising a good plan, in spite of the fact that we hadn't done this before. A couple of Ron's rangers showed up just as we were pulling out of the parking lot, so now we had a total of four people to assist in this project. Ron drove the truck and I followed in my El Camino vet truck in case we needed any meds from it. Ron and I both had radios for any emergency that might come up.

We stopped just inside the gate to Section III by the elephant house to finalize our game plan and to load the darts with M-99. Being near the elephant house and watching Damien go about his morning activities in the elephant yard still gave me chills and a sick feeling in the pit of my stomach. I guessed the fear would gradually subside in time, as would the soreness in my chest and ribs.

Damien leading his herd around the pen.

Damien looked like he was still in charge of the herd as he worked his way around the pen, checking on each member and making an occasional charge at anything that might threaten him from the outside. At his age, though, he would face challenges to his authority from several of the other males. As I observed them in the following months, I saw others who actually charged him and even tried to spar with him. The encounters were all brief, as Damien put them in their place with a forceful head butt or body block.

The elephants served only as a brief distraction, and after filling two darts with a mixture of M-99 and Rompun, we were ready to find our victims. M-99 (Etorphine) is the single most potent narcotic in the world. As little as 2 cc can immobilize a 3,000-pound rhino; as little as one drop can kill a human. It affects the central nervous system by putting the animal in a trance or stupor, and in larger doses it can stop the heart or respiration. Needless to say, I always wear gloves and am very careful in handling this product.

The Capes we were after weighed about 800 pounds each and would need a dose of 1 cc of M-99 and 1/2 cc Rompun. Rompun, or Xylazine, is a potent tranquilizer. When given in combination with the M-99, it allows you to use less of the M-99 and, more importantly, reduces the nervous effects, or pacing, that the animals go through in the initial excitatory phase of the immobilization. I felt that this drug would keep them standing and still allow us to get a rope on them, so we could walk them up in the trailer. It all sounded real good in theory.

Section III, where the cheetahs, rhino, Capes, and hippos were kept,

The Cape herd resting in Section III.

was a beautiful section. All of the vegetation and landscaping was natural, and very little had been done in the way of renovation. Numerous natural hills, or berms, had been created many years before by sand mining, and the resulting valleys around them had been overgrown by the thickest vegetation you could imagine. All of the tall trees had been kept intact, and two large lakes that also had been created by prior digging were absolutely beautiful in the middle of all of this natural jungle.

The animals were very much at home here, and it did my heart good to see them in their natural habitat, as opposed to concrete pens or some other zoo environment. The hope was that in this natural environment — created by the open, drive-through concept — the animals would feel at home enough to breed, thus preserving all exotics, especially the endangered species. That dream actually came true a year later when the cheetahs began breeding and giving birth to several litters right here in Section III of International Wildlife Park-Grand Prairie.

After making a couple of rounds and hunting unsuccessfully for the Capes, we stopped our vehicles on a rise a few yards from each other. Ron called me on the radio. "Hey, where do you think these guys are hidin'? We've been all over this section twice."

"I'm sure they're bedded down in some of those valleys an' simply don't want to be seen. Do we dare go through some of that thick stuff to try and flush them out?"

"Better not do that, Doc," he answered quickly.

"Well, what then?" I queried.

"I tell you what. Let's try putting out some feed on the road around the thickest parts and drive off for a while and see if they'll come out to eat."

"Sounds good!"

We dumped some feed at a promising location and left. After about 20 or 30 minutes of waiting by a lake, we started back up the roads, quietly and slowly, with me in the lead. We knew there were two adult cows in this section, one mature bull, and two yearlings. As I rounded the last curve and came into view of the feed, I could see both of the younger Capes in the road eating, but no adults were in sight.

This was too good to be true. All I had to do was get a dart in them, and we were basically home free. The youngsters didn't seem alarmed as they chomped on their feed and looked at me in disgust. They wished I wasn't around, but they weren't about to leave that feed. Ron's plan was working.

As I raised the gun to pop the first yearling, a large head with a huge set of horns became visible some 30 yards off the road in the brush, and it was probably a cow. I will never forget how natural and picturesque that Cape looked with the frosty breath pumping from the nostrils. I felt like

The female Cape watching anxiously.

I was on an African safari!

I took my shot, and the dart hit the first Cape square in the hip. He whirled, snorted, and hit the brush heading straight for the cow. Her head had not moved, but her glaring stare of concern said, "You better not be hurting my calf or you will pay." The second calf, a young female, was still eating but getting nervous, so I popped her. She also whirled, snorted, and hit the brush heading for her momma.

"All right, Ron, now what? I've got my job done, and both darts are in. How are you gonna load these guys?" I said it in a joking voice, but I was somewhat serious because I had no idea as to the next step. I figured we obviously had to get a rope on them in about 15 minutes or the drug would be at its maximum effect and they would be down. They also might wander off into the lake and drown if not found immediately.

"Well, Doc, from here there ain't but one thing to try and that's head-on and full bore."

"What do you mean?"

"I'll show you. Grab a lariat and follow me."

With that, Ron baled from his truck with his two guys, and they headed straight for that Cape's head that was still glaring and had not moved. They were yelling, screaming, throwing clods and rocks, and waving their ropes over their heads.

This doesn't look real great to me. But I grabbed my rope and joined in as I ran through the brush yelling and screaming, getting farther and farther from my truck. I started looking at every possible tree that could be climbed in the event of an emergency. When I got about 15 yards from the Cape's head, I heard her snort; then she turned and hit the brush. I could hear the grapevines and briars crackle and break as she bulldozed her way through the dense brush.

"I've got one!" Ron yelled. "The male is over here and still up."

"Put the rope on him and head back to the trailer," I yelled back. About that time I ran into a small clearing and there stood the other one, head down and drooling. She seemed to be in a stupor, so I figured the M-99 had done its job. I dropped a noose over her head and yelled for the other ranger to come help me.

We had been very lucky so far, and it looked like we were going to pull this off. There was no sign of the cow or the rest of the group as we neared the last thicket, so I began to feel even more confident about our safety and success. I had lost sight of Ron and his helper, but I knew they were nearby because I could occasionally hear them yelling and urging their calf forward. Our calf was moving forward nicely, with the ranger pushing from behind and me pulling forward on the rope.

I remember thinking, *only a few more feet an' we're out of the brush,* when I heard a loud snort in the thicket to my left. My heart sank!

That old familiar lump in my throat and the sick feeling in the pit of my stomach returned as I began to realize what was happening. As sure as I was standing there, that cow or the herd bull was coming to the rescue of their calves. I yelled at Ron, "Drop the rope and run for your life! We've got a problem."

That warning snort was all that saved the lives of Ron and his ranger, as well as myself and my ranger. We were all scrambling and running as best we could toward the trailer when that 2,000-pound momma came busting out of the brush in a full charge. All four of us hit the road about the same time.

We had one big problem, however. The cow was between us and the truck and trailer. Fortunately for us she was so mad she chose the red trailer to slam into instead of us. She hit the trailer so hard the wooden slats splintered from the impact. She then whirled and ran at Ron, but he had been given a few precious moments where he could dive between the trailer and the truck. She still got to him, though, knocking him completely on the other side. Meanwhile, his assistant had managed to jump into the pickup bed and was safe. Ron recovered and quickly joined him.

But then, I knew I was the one with the big problem. I literally had no place to go. The cow was destroying the trailer with every charge and would surely slam anything that moved. My assistant and I managed to keep the back of the trailer between her and us. We did not dare to make that final ten-yard jaunt to the pickup because she would be on us before we would get to the truck and we would surely be killed. Ron and the other ranger were throwing buckets and anything else they could at the cow, but that was only making her madder. Things were not looking good at this point.

In a last-ditch effort, I yelled at my helper, "I'm goin' to try an' circle her to distract her an' then head for the truck. When she comes for me, you run jump in the truck." I could only hope that I still had enough speed left over from my track days at Dublin High School to pull this off.

I bolted past her, and sure enough here she came with her head down in a full charge with killing on her mind. I ran in the brush a ways, and guess what? There wasn't a tree in sight. She was gaining on me because brush to her was only like tall grass to me. My only hope was to hit the road. I hurdled over some final bushes and made the fastest sprint of my high school track career toward what was left of the back of the trailer.

I knew getting on the trailer wouldn't work and I sensed I couldn't make it to the pickup, so I focused my escape on one thing: a small space beneath the trailer. There couldn't have been more than 24-inches between the trailer and the asphalt, but I was on the small side, 5 feet, 6 inches tall and weighing 135 pounds, so I figured it was this or nothing. As I hit the asphalt face first and began my final crawl-slide beneath the trailer, the cow was on top of me. I had hoped that she would hit the trailer again and not me, but that was not the case. She stepped on the back of my right calf with her hoof, and I could feel her massive head and horns in the small of my back as I literally crawled for my life. I was lodged halfway beneath the trailer with only my thighs, calves, and feet protruding. My forearms, elbows and stomach were bleeding from the asphalt impact, and the cow was slamming me and stepping on me with every breath.

My chest was beginning to hurt as my newly mended ribs were surely being torn loose again. I could hear Ron and the rangers yelling for me, but there was nothing they could do. My only hope was to make it a few more feet. I crawled and squirmed with every ounce of energy I had left in my body, but I just couldn't make the last few inches.

As it turned out, it was the cow herself who actually saved me. She began to back up and then charge, each time hitting the bottom of my feet with her head. With each blow, I was moved farther and farther beneath the trailer until I was able to finally pull my feet up past the frame.

I was safe! I didn't know the condition of my feet yet, but I could feel everything, and I was breathing and alive. God had spared me again.

Ron and his crew were panic stricken. They were yelling and screaming, "Doc, Doc, where are you? Are you all right?"

They had not seen me go under the trailer and felt sure that the cow had killed me. Ron had managed to get his radio out of the front of the truck and had radioed for help. I could hear them talking but had been too scared to speak. They basically had written me off, and you could imagine their surprise when they heard my voice.

"I'm all right. I'm down here under the trailer."

"Doc, we thought you were dead!" Ron shouted. "How in the world did you get under the trailer?"

"I had a little help. It was a pretty tight squeeze, and I'm stuck an' can't turn over."

"Just hold on, help is on its way. We're all goin' to be OK," Ron assured me.

The cow retreated to the brush, and I hoped she had found her two immobilized calves and was preoccupied with them. At that point I was certain the calves were lying down and I hoped the mother would stay with them until help arrived.

When the helpers got to the scene, they asked, "Where's Doc? Where's Doc?"

"Beneath the trailer and we gotta get him out!" Ron answered.

"No way!" somebody said.

I responded, "Oh, yeah, there is a way, and get me outta here and watch for that cow. She could be back any minute!"

Somebody soon figured out the obvious solution, which was for Ron to drive the pickup and trailer slowly forward about 10 feet. I was bruised and bleeding, my pants were torn, and I had a lot of gravel imbedded in my skin. But I could stand and walk so I was OK.

The ropes still were attached to the yearlings, and they were down flat on their side at the edge of the road. The cow had retreated even farther into the brush at the sight of extra help, who dragged the two yearlings into the trailer they had brought with them.

I somehow managed to give the M-50-50 reversal agent to each yearling, and they stood right up. We may have had a destroyed trailer and a beaten up veterinarian, but our two Cape buffalo were loaded for the Ohio shipment.

When was I ever going to learn animal behavior? Animals think, and they protect each other. This was the second time I had become a victim of this fact of nature.

CHAPTER 6

WEREWOLF

My first few months at the park had been nothing like what I had anticipated. I had visions of actually practicing veterinary medicine on these animals, not being mauled or possibly killed by them. Instead of numerous challenging surgeries and internal medical cases, I had almost been the main course for an African lion, been slam-dunked by an African elephant, and been beaten to the ground by a Cape buffalo that mopped up the asphalt with me. What was even more amazing was the fact that this all happened in Grand Prairie, Texas, and I didn't have to travel all the way to Africa for these privileges. I had to say that at this point I was having serious second thoughts about my decision to become a wildlife veterinarian. At the rate I was going, I wouldn't live to see my 30th birthday.

In the defense of the animals, however, my mind kept coming back to the same basic fact: it is not that they are mean or killers, but when you invade animals' territories or threaten their friends or young, you need to be prepared for the consequences.

Bill York must have sensed my concerns or doubts about my future, or maybe he just wanted to be sure he kept a veterinarian on staff. At any rate, he echoed over the radio in that thick, English brogue, "Dr. Cannon, come in please."

"Go ahead," I replied.

"Doc, could you come to my office, please?"

"Sure, be right up." Within minutes I drove to Bill's office and went inside to see what bizarre job he had planned for me.

"Joe, how have you been doing? Had a couple of close calls, I hear."

"You might say that. I've been wondering if I'm really cut out for this or not."

"You're doing great, Joe. You're a natural, and I think what you need is a short vacation. When you come back, you need to spend more time on the medical aspect of the park and not so much on the capture and animal shipment."

It was like he had almost read my mind. "Where am I goin', Bill, and what's on tap for when I get back?"

"We have a white rhino shipment coming into New York next week, and I would like you and James Ashe to travel up there, bring them through quarantine, and make sure they get home safely. We have 12 in all that will be arriving. They have been on a boat for about three weeks, and I'm sure they will need antibiotics and physicals prior to moving them on down to Texas. Joe, don't worry. All of these are in a very safe rhino crate so they shouldn't be able to hurt you."

"Oh, I'm sure they'll find a way." I managed a weak smile.

"You'll be gone about 10 days, and when you get back I have a project for you."

"What kind of project?" I asked cautiously.

"It's one that will challenge your surgical skills to their fullest." He had that familiar sly grin on his face.

"OK, tell me more. What's goin' on?"

"I'll tell you this much. It involves cosmetic surgery on that old ugly lion out in Section II we call Werewolf."

"I remember him. He's the one with his lower lip saggin' down and all the scars from the lionesses beating up on him."

"Exactly, but the problem is that we aren't having any cubs being born, and Werewolf is our only mature breeding male right now."

"I understand your problem, but I really don't see where I can help you solve it."

"Joe, animals are just like people in a lot of ways. If you can figure out a way to make this ugly lion more attractive, I think the females will more readily accept him. Not to mention the fact that he will be able to eat better, groom himself better, and feel better about himself in general. If we can just stop him from drooling on himself, that's got to make him feel better."

I sort of stared at Bill in a questioning manner before he responded, "Have faith, Joe, and bone up on your cosmetic surgery."

"OK, Bill, you're the expert on animal behavior, not me. I'll have to trust you on this one."

After I left his office, I went directly to the lion hut where Werewolf was kept to get one final look at my new project before I left for New York.

I really wasn't sure if Bill was serious about this or just giving me a project so I could utilize my surgical skills and have something more gratifying to do. In either case, I decided to at least look at the poor creature to see if I felt I could help to improve his physical appearance.

I had been noticing this cat during my daily rounds, and he really was a wreck. His face was the worst part of his appearance — so grotesque that I felt sorry for him. The name Werewolf was appropriate: his lower lip sagged so badly that his canine teeth were never hidden, and he always had what looked like a constant snarl on his face. His ears had been practically chewed off, and what was left of one ear was hanging down lower than the other. His eyelids were torn, his face marked with deep scars from many fights with females, and he was simply pathetic. He would lie around most of the time and seldom compete for his share of the food when it was provided; therefore, he had become thin due to a state of partial malnutrition.

Bill had given me a project that might not be possible to complete, but I was game to try just about anything. I would give it my best. At least Werewolf would give me something to think about during my trip to and from New York.

They were flying me up there, and I was to ride back with the shipment in case there was a problem, like an animal getting out of the crate. On the following morning I packed my luggage and my medical bag, which included the dart gun and M-99, and drove to the airport. I met up with Jim, and we began discussing a plan to get these 3,500-pound creatures through quarantine and trucked to Grand Prairie. Jim had a lot of prior experience in shipping and receiving animals during his tenure at the International Animal Exchange Park in South Africa, so I felt very much at ease about the entire project.

I hadn't flown much at all prior to this trip and I certainly had never been to New York. I was looking forward to both with a great deal of enthusiasm. The flight, while exciting for me, was uneventful, but it did give me the opportunity to think about the surgery that was waiting for me when I got back. I already had several ideas on how to reconstruct Werewolf's face and was looking forward to the challenge.

The white rhino, distinguished by their large square lips, were fast becoming extinct and currently on the endangered species list, as were the cheetahs. It was the hope of everyone that both the rhino and cheetahs would breed while in their new home in Section III, with its thick undergrowth, trees, rolling hills, and natural lakes. Once these magnificent creatures roamed free, together in their beautiful and natural habitat, it would be a sight to see.

The rhino were being held in quarantine at a large warehouse near docks owned by Lykes Steamship Lines. The warehouse was set up and supervised by the USDA and was under tight security. Fortunately for us the quarantine period had ended the day before we arrived, and all Jim and I had to do was get through security and inspect the animals to make sure they were ready to ship to Texas.

"Isn't this a grand sight, Doc? To see this many white rhino assembled in one area is unbelievable."

"And since I've never even seen a white rhino up close," I answered, "this really is a first for me."

Remarkably, there weren't a lot of sounds made by these animals. You could hear the crates creak when they would shift their weight and occasionally a loud bang when one would slam into the front of the crate, which was really more of a metal-like sound. As I looked closer I could see that the fronts and backs of the crates were made with 4-inch pipe with 10- to 12-inch gaps between them. This managed to keep them safely in the crate, yet allowed them room to feed and clean. The major parts of the crates were made of heavy-duty 4-by-12-inch shiplap, plenty strong enough to hold these prehistoric-looking monsters in place.

"Those Africans build a good crate, eh Doc?"

"Thank God. We sure don't need any more animal problems or emergencies."

Jim and I began the inspection we came to do. As we were going from crate to crate, a lady and her young daughter came up to Jim and asked if her daughter could have her picture made with the rhino and us. They were the family of one of the dockworkers. It was certainly all right with us, if the port authorities didn't have a problem with it. After checking with them and getting permission, we chose a crate and walked to the front where a very large rhino horn was protruding between the bars.

As Jim reached out and touched the horn, he looked at me. "You know, Doc, this is not a horn at all, but a type of compressed hair."

"You're kiddin' me," I said with surprise.

"Not at all. Feel of it," he urged.

As I touched that horn, I felt that a permanent connection had been made between Africa and Texas. I could not believe this huge mammal just stood there and allowed me to feel his horn and examine his eyes and muzzle. The little girl also was able to touch him, and I'm sure she will remember that forever.

Rhino in quarantine in New York.

As we continued our exam, I noticed a couple of rhino had a mucus discharge coming from their noses. Jim and I decided that we might as well give all of them a large injection of Flocillin in order to prevent any shipping fever that might occur on their way to Texas. As I got out my syringes, needles, and antibiotics, I noticed Jim looking at me with a sly grin on his face as I began to draw up the medication into the syringes.

"Doc, what are you gonna do with those scrawny needles?" he asked in his South African accent, even more pronounced than usual.

"Won't work, I take it."

"These guys have skin in the range of two inches thick in places and a regular needle won't even get through the skin, not to mention get into the muscle."

I felt really embarrassed with my regular needles and looked to him for help. "What do we do now?"

"Try these," he said as he produced several needles from a small box in his bag. These needles were at least 4 inches long and 14-gauge. They had a stylet (a wire) to use when injecting to keep a skin plug from stopping up the needle. "These are what we used in South Africa, and they work very well."

I was glad to have them and eager to try them out. We went about injecting approximately 120 ml of Flocillin into each rhino. Even with the longer, heavier needle it was very difficult to penetrate their thick skin. Surprisingly, however, they moved very little as the needle was inserted and the medication was pushed into their massive bodies. All went well, and before we knew it we were through and it was time to start loading them on the flatbed trailers.

It was during the loading process that I found out that South Africans and New York unionized dockworkers didn't get along well. I could tell by the look on Jim's face that he was not pleased with the rapid speed at which the dockworkers approached, lifted, and moved the large crates with the huge rhino inside. Things had gone too smoothly, so I guessed it was time for something to go wrong.

Jim knew that if the crates were not picked up exactly in the center, a shift of weight could end in disaster. He was getting increasingly nervous and annoyed with the manner in which each crate was being dropped onto the flatbeds, and he asked them several times to slow down and be more careful. He even went to the supervisor of the workers, but nothing could alter their work habits.

Then it happened!

As one of the forklift drivers approached a crate from the side, he misjudged where the iron skids and the wood came together and rammed the forks through the wood and into the crate itself. He hit it with such force that the forks came out on the other side, splintering wood everywhere. Then, amazingly, he continued the loading process by lifting the forks, which resulted in both sides of the crate being torn out as the forks came to rest against the stomach of the rhino.

Now we had a ripped up crate and a mad rhino suspended in midair, some 10 feet above the concrete floor of the warehouse. Jim's skin started to turn a deep red, and I knew we were in trouble.

"You idiot!" Jim yelled at the top of his lungs. "I warned you to slow down and watch what you were doin'!" Jim turned to me, "Doc, grab the dart gun and load a dart with M-99. That rhino will be loose in here in a few minutes at the rate these idiots are goin'."

I grabbed my kit and began making up a dart. The forklift driver, finally realizing what he had done and angry at Jim for yelling at him, simply turned off the lift with the crate elevated in the air and shouted a few obscenities in Jim's direction before walking away.

"Are you just gonna leave him there to die?" Jim yelled back.

"You can load him yourself as far as I'm concerned," the driver shouted as he disappeared out a door.

By that time I had the dart loaded and was ready for anything. Jim jumped on the forklift, cranked it up, and began slowly lowering the crate to the ground. Once the pressure was off of the rhino, we were able to assess the damage and quiet the scared animal. His legs and the ventral abdomen were cut, but miraculously that was all the damage we could see. The crate was beyond repair but not torn up enough that the animal could escape. All in all, we had been lucky.

I began cleaning and spraying the cuts and Jim was fortunate enough to locate an empty rhino crate that had been sent over on the boat in case of an emergency. By this time, Jim had given up on the dockworkers and was zipping all over the dock on the forklift. He never missed a beat. He placed the new crate in front of the torn one, and we were able to ease the rhino gently into the new crate.

At that point all we needed was to load the remaining rhino onto the flatbed. Well, guess what? The dockworkers were suddenly refusing to work. As it turned out, it was probably better that Jim finished the loading because he did a good job and did it slowly and carefully. Several hours later we had our cargo and were leaving New York. We definitely had dodged a bullet and were thankful to be on the road home.

After an uneventful trip back to Grand

Kurt preparing to un-crate rhino in Texas.

Unloading rhino in Section III.

Happy rhino in his new Texas home.

Prairie and with the rhino safe in Section III, I was ready to test my surgical skills on Werewolf. As I stood in front of his cage for a second time trying to decide on the best approach, I began to realize the challenge confronting me with this surgery. Werewolf hadn't changed any in the week I had been gone except maybe he had gotten a little thinner and received a few more scratches.

The old monarch had a look in his eyes that he just didn't care anymore and had given up. When he tried to groom himself, he just drooled all over everything and basically made a disgusting mess. I felt really sorry for him and hoped I could help him. I also decided to try some hormone therapy on him with the hope that it might help him grow a mane and put on some much needed weight. With a surgical plan in mind, I scheduled Werewolf for surgery the following day.

As I entered the hospital room the next morning, I was greeted by Fred Coston, our public relations director, and two reporters from the *Dallas Morning News*. I sure hadn't planned on an audience, but I guessed Fred had leaked the story to his cronies at the newspaper, and they figured it would make an interesting article. I pulled Fred over to the side and informed him that they could take photos for the paper but they would not be allowed in the operating room. He reluctantly agreed but was

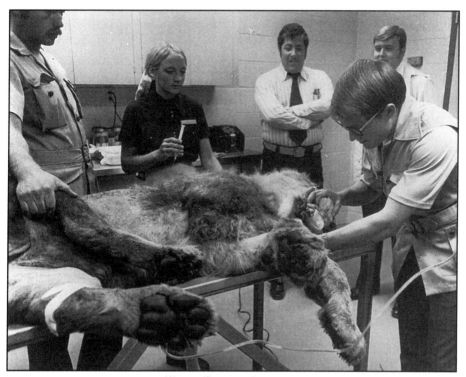

Werewolf's cosmetic surgery.

pleased that they could take before and after shots, and they were happy to do the story.

Well, it looked like Werewolf was going to become famous; that really put the pressure on me to make this thing work.

With everything ready in the surgery room, I walked up to the crate where Werewolf was awaiting his anesthetic. When the dart — loaded with 15 ml Ketamine (a general anesthetic) and ace (short for acepromazine, a tranquilizer) — hit him in his hip, he whirled and roared as if to let me know that he still had some spunk left. It was good to see this aggression, which gave me hope that we might be able to help him. Once we had him asleep, we transferred him to a scale. His 425 pounds was about 300 pounds less than what he should have weighed. We had a long way to go.

As I surveyed the face and lower lip of this anesthetized cat, I noticed the keloidal scar tissue was much larger and more extensive than I had anticipated. It not only involved his lip area, extending into the gum line, but also covered some of his lower teeth. This could explain his difficulty in grooming, as well as biting and chewing his food. The scar tissue was about the size of a tennis ball and was obviously going to have to be removed. The lip could then be pulled back up and reattached in its appropriate place.

It took about one to one-and-one-half hours of dissection to remove the keloidal tissue in its entirety and another half-hour to reattach his lower lip to the jaw. Werewolf was doing fine on all of his vitals, so I decided to go ahead and remove the deep, ugly scars on his face. After nearly three-and-one-half hours, it was time to stop the surgery and wake him up. I had to say that he looked amazingly well, and I really felt like we had helped him. I quickly added his hormone injections as he was coming around, and then he went back to the dens for a two-week recuperation and healing process.

Bill York called me on the radio two days later to tell me that Werewolf didn't look like the same cat, and we should consider changing his name to Romeo.

This made me feel good, and I really felt there was some hope for the old cat after all. I didn't know if it was the surgery or the hormones, or maybe a combination of both, but Werewolf seemed to thrive over the next few months. He not only was able to eat and drink better, but he developed a ferocious growl and even grew a slightly thicker mane. He was a much more pleasant-looking cat and was observed grooming himself on a regular basis. He gained weight and eventually was back to his old fighting weight of 700 pounds. Life was good for Werewolf!

About four months following the surgery, Bill decided it was time to turn one of our best lionesses in with him to see if she would possibly accept him. Bill thought she might be in heat so this would be a good test. "It's the only way we're ever going to know if she will accept him or try to kill him," reasoned Bill.

I supported his decision. "I'll be standing by with my dart if she chooses fighting." I'll never know if she had just forgotten who he was or if she didn't recognize him as that pathetic old cat she used to beat up, but this time it was love at first sight.

Bill was ecstatic at the possibility of having some baby "Werewolfs" around and made it a point to give all of the females a chance to date this new Romeo. The courtships really paid off, and it wasn't long before we had lion cubs everywhere. Over the next year, we actually had a surplus of cubs and furnished them to other parks as they opened across the United States.

As for Werewolf, he would later succumb to a liver disease and old age, but not without leaving a legacy that would last forever. I felt certain that Werewolf died a happy and contented cat, as he was able to live the later part of his life with some dignity.

Werewolf's first cub.

CHAPTER 7

ELLIE AND JERRY

With Werewolf's surgery behind me and with my doing more and more medical oriented work every day, I too felt like the old monarch as my confidence slowly started to come back. I still respected the fact that any of these animals had the capability to seriously hurt me, but I was losing my fear and enjoyed my work immensely. Every day was a new experience with a different animal.

Section I was home to over two hundred head of various African and American antelope-like species. Even with a few North American elk roaming around, all the animals got along amazingly well. One of the cow elk had just calved the day before, and mother and baby were doing fine.

I was surprised, to say the least, when Craig Collvins, a new ranger, boomed over the radio, "Come in, Doc! Come in somebody! We have a problem in Section I."

"Where are you?" I asked anxiously.

"By the lake," came back the frantic voice.

"What's goin' on?"

"I've got an adult Nilgai cow tryin' to stomp our new elk calf."

"I'm on my way." I grabbed my capture equipment and jumped into my truck. As I rounded the last corner by the lake, I could still see the Nilgai cow trying to get to the baby elk and Craig and Ron trying to keep her off of the calf. Not wasting any time, I quickly made a dart and popped the Nilgai with 3 cc of M-99. That'll stop her for a while.

As the Nilgai lay down, I yelled to Ron and Craig to grab the baby and meet me at the nursery. I could tell from a distance that she had some serious problems. After reversing the Nilgai with M-50-50, I raced back to the hospital to assess the damage to the baby. I had never been this close to a baby elk, and she was definitely something special. As she looked up at me with those huge brown eyes, it was love at first sight.

I then began the exam, only to find that she had not one, but two broken legs. Her right front and right rear legs had compound fractures with bones protruding from the skin in the centers of both legs. The Nilgai had really done a number on her.

Since she was only one or two days old and her breaks were severe, my colleagues suggested euthanasia; raising an orphan on a bottle would be a big challenge, even if the fractures healed nicely. When I drew up the euthanasia solution and started to inject it into the jugular vein, I made the mistake of looking into those big brown eyes again and it was all over.

"I can't do this, guys," I admitted weakly, trying to hold back the tears. "I thought I could, but I can't."

Everyone in the room sighed with relief; for the time being at least, I knew I had made the right decision. "What the heck," I added. "If you all are willing to feed her four times a day for the next couple of months, I'll try my best to fix these fractures."

They all agreed they would take turns, so we had an orphan elk on our hands.

As it turned out, I was able to repair the fractures by using stainless steel pins. The pins were surgically placed into the center of the bones,

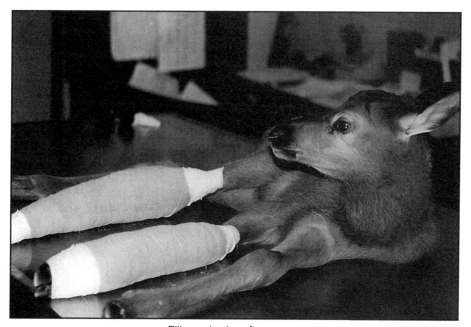

Ellie awakening after surgery.

and the muscles were repaired and sutured back together. Finally, a heavy-duty cast was placed on each leg to give support.

We named her Ellie. She got stronger each day, and after about 30 days of helping her up and down, she was able to stand on her own. The casts were changed at the end of 60 days and removed at the end of 90 days. The legs had healed unbelievably well. It was so rewarding over the next few weeks to see her playing in the nursery yard. I felt especially good about the game management concept of which we were all a part, since in the wild Ellie would have been certain prey for a mountain lion or would have died from infection or shock. As it turned out, she lived seven more years and birthed four beautiful calves.

Only a week after Ellie's injury, Craig yelled again on the radio. "Come in, Doc. I need to show you somethin' in Section I." Something had to be wrong, but he didn't sound as excited as he had been with Ellie.

"On my way, Craig."

When I met Craig in Section I, I didn't see anything obviously wrong. Craig hopped in my truck and said, "Hey, let's go look at a bongo down here. I think he has a small problem." When he mentioned the word "bongo," he got my attention since this type of African antelope was not only endangered but worth about $50,000 each.

"I hope it's nothin' too serious because you know what they cost. York will have a cow," I told him.

"I just don't like the way her horn is growing toward her head. It looks like it's about to puncture her eye or stick into her head," Craig explained.

I was a little surprised at the detail that this new ranger was giving about his observations, and it was very good to have someone so conscientious on staff. As we stood at the bongo pens and looked at our patient, I was amazed at how accurate Craig had been. Her left horn was curled back, mere millimeters from the bottom portion of the eye. We had received these animals only the week before, and no one, including myself, had spotted the problem.

"Craig, it's great that you caught this. Could've been a big problem in a few weeks."

"Can we fix it, Doc?"

"I think so. All we have to do is immobilize her with M-99 and sort of dehorn her or saw the tip off."

Bill York was elated that our staff, mainly Craig, had found this problem and gave his immediate consent to immobilize and dehorn the bongo. After calling the insurance company and alerting them about our plans, we set up the immobilization for early the next morning. We did a lot of immobilizations early to beat the heat and make it easier on the stressed animal.

Horn removal with Gigli wire.

Around daylight the next morning, Craig and Ron Surratt met me at the bongo pen. I gave our patient 2 cc of M-99, and about seven minutes later we were able to get our hands on her. Using a piece of Gigli wire, I was able to remove about half of the curved-down horn. I reversed her with M-50-50, and she came up well. Although she looked a little different from a normal bongo, she was able to grow, flourish, and eventually become a producing cow. This was another glowing credit to the game park theme and the reproduction of endangered species.

The challenges of treating the animals, however, continued at a steady pace.

It was just the following week when Craig called to tell me that Jerry, one of the largest male giraffe, was limping badly.

I guess Craig is goin' to keep me busy all year doin' immobilizations. I was almost afraid to look at Jerry because I hadn't immobilized a giraffe yet, and I figured he would probably need it. "Craig, you're wearin' me out," I joked. "What are you goin' to find next?"

"Just doin' my job, Doc," he laughed.

"I know, and you're doing it well."

Jerry was about 17 feet tall and weighed about 2,000 pounds. He was a huge, mature giraffe. While looking at him with Craig, I could see that he was definitely lame. His left front leg was swollen in the hoof area, and he would hardly touch it to the ground.

"He's got to have a foot abscess, Craig. I bet he's stepped on a piece of wire or glass."

"What do you do, Doc?" came the old familiar question from Craig.

"He's got to be immobilized and that foot examined and possibly opened up."

"This ought to be good. Have you ever done one of these?"

"This will be my first one, but we can do it."

That night I referred to Dr. Fowler's book on exotic animal medicine and surgery, finding a short paragraph on giraffe immobilization. It seemed their biggest problem was hyper excitability while being immobilized, which caused regurgitation. To reduce the chances of this happening, I decided to first give a tranquilizer before the M-99 knockdown. The combination of drugs would allow me to use less M-99, which is the primary cause of vomiting. I hoped that I could then get a rope on the head to prevent it from hitting the ground too hard. It all sounded good in theory, and it had to be tried since Jerry was probably going to lose his leg from infection if we didn't treat it.

Even to this day, immobilizing giraffe is not done on a routine basis due to their size and the difficulty of preventing injury during the laying down procedure. Imagine the impact of a 17-foot tall, 2,000-pound pole toppling to the ground. The immobilization was scheduled for the following morning due to the summer heat we were experiencing.

Early the next morning I popped Jerry with 1 cc of Rompun, a horse and cow tranquilizer. I gave it about 15 minutes to work and after his head was lowered and he was salivating slightly, I gave 2 cc of M-99. To

Step 1 of Jerry's immobilization.

Step 2 and 3 of Jerry's immobilization. Roping him to prevent injury as he lays down.

my surprise, Jerry remained upright in spite of both drugs but seemed to be in a stupor. He ambled over into a corner and just stood there, pressing on the fence and trying to go forward.

Now what? How will I ever get him down to look at his leg?

"Let's just rope him an' then pull him over," Craig suggested.

Since I didn't have a better plan, I grabbed my lariat and decided to do it "Texas style." When we got the rope secure around his throat, we all began the chore of pulling Jerry back and over, trying to break his fall with padded supports. The tranquilizer idea was working well; Jerry remained still enough to allow all of this manipulation, and he finally toppled over, hitting the ground with a thud.

I then walked up to this giant of nature, and as I touched and examined his leg I could hardly contain my excitement. To be so close to something this awesome gave me goose bumps. After a few brief moments of marveling at his beauty, I began my examination and treatment in earnest.

87

The left front foot was extremely swollen, and when I touched it I could feel it was very hot. In addition, I could feel a very prominent digital pulse. The symptoms added up to an abscess, but the problem was going to be in finding it. As I probed and mashed all around on the sole, I could find no puncture or obvious cut. Jerry's sole was the size of a dinner plate, so there was a lot of surface area to inspect.

Just as I was about to give up, I felt a slightly roughened area located in the middle of the sole. At first I thought it was a thick piece of tissue, but as I moved my fingers back and forth, I found that it was too sharp for that. I decided to examine this area with my hoof knife, and, sure enough, I found what appeared to be the end of a wire. It was a piece of good old Texas baling wire.

I hollered at Craig, "Bring me a pair of pliers as quick as you can."

Craig laughed. "Doc, he's not a bale of hay, so what are you goin' to do with pliers?"

"Just bring the pliers and I'll show you." With pliers in hand, I struggled with the end of the wire. I was amazed after pulling it out since it was more than three inches long. Pus and infection shot everywhere, so I knew I had found the problem.

Ron and Craig looked at the wire in disbelief. "No wonder he was limping." Ron was as amazed as I was.

"What would have happened out in the wild if he had a foot infection an' wasn't treated?" Craig asked.

"In time he would have been dinner for a lion or hyena. He would not have gotten over this type of infection, an' it would have eventually killed him."

So far, fate had smiled on us. We had managed to sedate Jerry safely and had located his problem. All we had to do then was finish his treatment and get him back on his feet. I deepened the abscessed wire wound in order to drain off a lot more infection. Next I gave him about 120 cc of penicillin and a tetanus shot. I also put on a wrap to cover the bottom of the foot. We were ready to give him the antidote that would get him back on his feet.

As I slowly injected 2 cc of M-50-50 into his vein, his breathing increased immediately, and he blinked his eyes. It couldn't have gone smoother. Jerry slowly sat up on his brisket and then started his assent.

I didn't think he would ever get those long legs unwrapped from behind him, but when he did he stood upright. I noticed as he walked away that he was already putting full weight on the injured foot.

It was amazing how quickly he responded to the treatment. Jerry improved rapidly over the next few days and before long he was back with his group, doing whatever giraffe do.

Jerry in lateral recumbency while working on foot.

Surgery on foot is completed and Jerry is getting back on his feet.

89

CHAPTER 8

SQUEAKY

The wildlife park was doing well. Most of the animals had adapted nicely to their new home and, more importantly, they appeared happy. As the months passed, I was feeling better about my new job and not only did I really look forward to coming to work each day, but I also felt like I was making a difference in the world and playing an important role in wildlife preservation. We all felt that the open, drive-through park concept was definitely working.

We had seen several of the species breeding, but it was too early to have any babies. Our biggest hopes for reproduction lay in Section III, which was such a natural environment that we had expectations of raising both rhino and cheetahs. Up to that point, only a handful of white rhino had been born in captivity and only one or two litters of cheetahs. We wanted to change that.

But our hopes became somewhat dampened one day when Ron came driving up to the nursery with a cheetah crate in the back. "We've got a problem, Doc," he announced anxiously. "I think a car has run over Squeaky and her leg may be broken. She looks like she's in pretty bad shape."

"It sure looks broken," I said as I looked into the crate and noticed her labored breathing and extremely swollen leg. "Let's get her into the clinic immediately."

No one had actually seen a car hit her, but since this was a drive-through park, the cheetahs could come up very close to the cars. All of the signs of a possible fracture were there — bruising, limping, swelling, tenderness, etc. Of all the cheetahs, Squeaky was the most calm and would on occasion let you touch her. Her actual name was J.J., but we nicknamed her Squeaky because of the squeaky noises she would make when she wanted attention.

Due to her pain, however, I elected to go ahead and sedate her by using a syringe pole. This would relax her, relieve her pain, and make it safer for everyone who would be handling her. I gave her 3 cc of Ketamine with 1 cc of ace IM (intramuscularly).

After we were able to get her relaxed, we moved her out of the crate and onto the surgery table. Her vital signs were stable, but her temperature was 104 degrees. I was sure that the combination of her pain, stress, and the heat had caused the temperature spike. As she began to relax in the air-conditioned room, her temperature came down to normal range. She was slightly dehydrated and a little shaky, so I started her on IV fluids. As I examined her rear leg, it was obvious that she had a mid-shaft femur fracture.

"Let's get an x-ray of this leg. I know it's broken, but we need to see if it's fixable." My assistant, Craig, wheeled in our portable x-ray machine, and in only minutes we had an answer. "Clean break in mid-shaft femur," I noted. "I believe it is treatable."

It was logical to go ahead and fix the leg since Squeaky was already anesthetized and on fluids. I had some large stainless steel IM pins on hand, and it appeared that one in particular would fit. After performing two hours of surgery, I felt that I had the leg secure. The bone ends had gone back together well, and since I was dealing with a cheetah here, I decided to put on a large Thomas splint to minimize movement and rotation. As it turned out, this kept Squeaky from tearing around the compound before the bone had healed and possibly refracturing the leg. With the surgery over, I pulled some blood for routine tests and placed Squeaky back in her crate to recover.

"What are these bone-lookin' things in her stomach?" asked Craig as he cleverly held up the x-ray to the light.

"Oh, you can read x-rays now?" I asked jokingly.

"It looks like she's eaten a rat or something with all of these bones in here," my clever, young assistant observed.

"OK, you've got me, Dr. Craig. Show me what you're talkin' about."

"Right here." He pointed to the center of the x-ray.

"Let me see that!" I grabbed the film from him, and I couldn't believe my eyes. Lo and behold, right there on the film that I was looking at were seven baby cheetah skeletons. I was in shock!

"Craig, Squeaky is pregnant. Guess I'm gonna have to let you read all the x-rays from now on," I added sheepishly. "If it hadn't been for you, we wouldn't have known Squeaky is a mother-to-be."

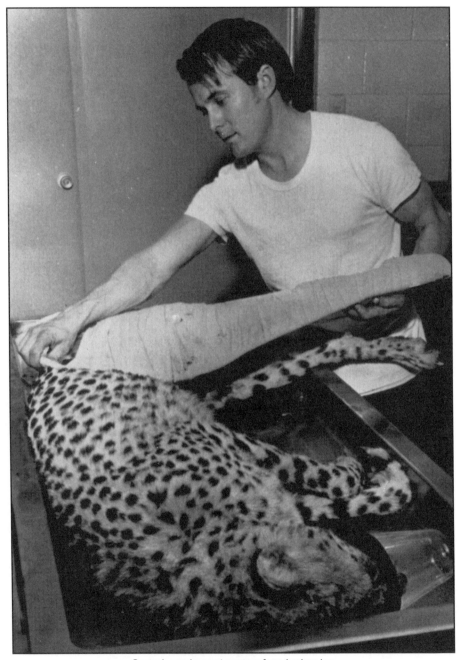

Squeaky underwent surgery for a broken leg.

I had been so wrapped up in looking at the broken bone that I completely overlooked the tiny skulls and skeletons. Craig was beaming and strutting around as the entire clinic became alive with excitement about the news of the upcoming birth of the park's first endangered species.

As I carefully studied the x-rays, my heart pounded. I felt like an expectant father. During the previous year I had developed a close relationship with several of the animals in the park, and Squeaky was one of the closest. On occasion she had walked up to me, made her familiar squeaking noises, and let me touch her on the head.

I just couldn't believe it! Our Squeaky was going to have one of the first litters of cheetah cubs in captivity.

I was able to determine from looking at the maturity of the tiny skeletons that she was not far from giving birth. My next obvious concern was how the stress of the injury and the surgery had affected the cubs. With all that Squeaky had been through, there was certainly a chance that she could abort or give birth and have no milk. Since she was so far along in her gestation and would need the Thomas splint for at least six weeks, we decided to keep her in a hospital room for close observation.

During this time Squeaky and I became even closer. I would even feed her the special vitamin-meat mixture from my hand. Although she occasionally felt threatened and would spit and paw at me, she always came back affectionately with her little squeaking noises. She tolerated the cast well and even learned to walk with it, using it as a crutch.

She looked fine, but she wasn't developing any milk, and I was becoming worried. We were feeding her extra meat and Zupreme (a cooked, canned, chicken-based feline diet), but it wasn't helping. We started her on powder-type feline milk in an attempt to stimulate milk production. She was fairly young, and this being her first litter didn't help the situation either.

Squeaky had been in the hospital room for about 14 days when I noticed a distinct change in her behavior. She became very standoffish, and her appetite decreased. I knew she was getting close to having her babies. I still couldn't detect much mammary development, but there would be time for her milk to come down even after birth. My colleagues and I discussed maintaining a 24-hour watch from that point on, but decided against it since it might make her nervous and do more harm than good.

As I arrived at her door the following morning, I knew something was different when she didn't meet me as usual. I opened the door and went into the room to check on her and was greeted by a different cheetah.

Squeaky glared at me, growling and spitting, with the hair along the top of her back standing straight up. I froze, my heart was pounding, and I was terrified. I knew I couldn't turn my back on her, and I wasn't sure if I had time to back up.

Then she charged me! Luckily her charge ended right at my feet, which allowed me time to quickly back out of the door. However, not knowing anyone was behind me, I backed straight into Kay, our hospital nursery manager.

"What's wrong with you?" she asked. "You look like you've seen a ghost!"

I took a deep breath. "I'm not real sure, but I'd say we have some cubs since Squeaky just tried to eat me."

"Are you all right?"

"I'm fine," I gasped. "Just a little weak in the knees right now."

After sitting down for a minute and gaining my composure, I was ready to try again, but this time with much more caution. Kay and I had provided some clean coastal Bermuda hay for Squeaky to use as a bed, and I was fairly certain the cubs were nestled down in the hay. As we carefully opened the door and shined a light back into the corner, we could see Squeaky lying down and apparently licking something. We put feed and water in for her and left her alone. With any luck, she would become less protective in a few days, and we could get a better look at her and the cubs. We could only hope that they had enough milk to survive until then.

Two days passed, and every time Kay or I looked in on Squeaky she was licking her babies. We naturally assumed all was well. On the third day, however, we heard the whining of the cubs as they nursed, or were trying to be fed.

Squeaky was not eating well, so I was getting nervous. I didn't know if she had delivered all the cubs, if they were getting enough milk, or if she still had one or two cubs or afterbirths inside.

Anything was possible, and I could only rely on the fact that Mother Nature usually takes care of her own. I certainly didn't want to interfere and cause more problems. As I wondered what to do, my mind drifted back to Silky Harris and how if I had not interfered he would have starved to death in his den.

By day four, I couldn't take it any longer. As my dad would have said, "Do somethin' even if it's wrong." I told my assistant, "Kay, get the blow-dart kit and the immobilization equipment. We're not goin' to wait any longer."

Kay acted a little reluctant as she left to gather up the items, and when she returned, she asked, "Are you sure about this?"

"No, I'm not sure at all. How can we be? But there are too many unanswered questions here, and I'm not goin' to stand idly by any longer."

My plan was to blow-dart Squeaky and, after she was sedated, to conduct a thorough exam, including pulling blood for a complete blood profile. At the same time, I could examine the cubs and check them for dehydration and any other signs of sickness.

When the blow-dart sank into Squeaky's right hip, she whirled and let out a combination growl and scream that I didn't think could possibly come from her. She grabbed the plastic dart in her teeth, jerked it out, and slung it against the wall as if to say, "How dare you do that to me!"

The dart did its work, however, and within two or three minutes she was starting to wobble and stagger. Five minutes later she was completely down. Her temperature was normal and she appeared fine, but I drew blood anyway to establish a good baseline for healthy cheetahs in the event that we ever had to compare this blood work to an abnormal one.

When I examined her mammary development, I became very concerned. She did have some milk but not enough for all her cubs.

As Kay and I crept toward the moving straw, we were both shaking with excitement, knowing we were about to touch some of the first cheetahs ever born in captivity. Their little eyes were still glued tightly shut as we reached out to examine the small, furry objects with spots. We got quite a start, however, when the first one spit and hissed at us, and then the others followed his lead. How could they tell that we weren't their mother when they were only three days old and their eyes were shut? I felt it was just another tribute to Mother Nature and what I'd call the wild factor.

If our count was complete, there were seven of these little, furry and spotted creatures, all of them hissing and spitting to their hearts' content, and not one bit happy about being handled. Most of them were amazingly fat and sassy, with the exception of two, who were both very dehydrated and already showing signs of weakness. These two poor babies would even fall over when trying to walk, and it appeared that the five stronger cubs were pushing the two weaker ones aside and gobbling up all of what milk there was. I was glad I acted when I did. One more day and it would have probably been too late.

Kay must have read my mind as she watched me examine the cubs. "Doc, I know what you're thinking, and I'll be honest with you. I've never raised cheetah cubs on a bottle and I'm not sure I want the responsibility, considering this is an endangered species and there's pressure to make it work."

"I understand, Kay, but someone has to do it and we're it. Not only could it be lifesaving for the two runts, it could also be lifesaving for the other five since they would have more milk to divide among themselves." With all of this explained, I handed the runts to Kay. After a final inspection of Squeaky, we turned off the light to allow our new mother some peace and quiet as she came out of the anesthesia.

We quickly found that the new cubs were an absolute joy to be around and to feed on the bottle. Since the cubs had not received much colostrum from their mother's milk, they had their share of diarrhea and upper respiratory infections. Despite a few setbacks, we still managed to raise two healthy, cheetah cubs to adulthood.

Squeaky did her part, too, by becoming a mother again to all seven in about four months. We had the neatest litter of young cheetahs you could imagine.

The press coverage and public relations that we received from our new additions were invaluable to our marketing department. Not only were the newspapers constantly calling to monitor their progress, but the entire zoological community wanted specific details about how the cheetahs were kept, their diet, and so much more.

I maintain to this day that our roam-free environment had as much to do with the breeding success as anything.

CHAPTER 9

BIG DADDY

With the cheetahs breeding program in full swing, it had started to look like Section III was going to be a smashing success. It was definitely our most rugged section; and the concept of running cheetahs, white rhino, hippo, and Cape buffalo together seemed to be working. Not only did we have a healthy litter of cheetah cubs, we had two or three white rhino that were getting mammary development and were coming close to calving. I thought that the animals being in direct contact with other species gave them a feeling of security that they were at home in Africa.

Life was good! I loved my job and was gaining still more confidence in my ability to treat exotics. Little did I know, however, that I was about to face one of the biggest challenges of my career, and that it would again involve Section III.

"Doc! Doc, come in please," came a frantic cry over the two-way radio. "John Clay here; you need to come down to Section III immediately. I already have the section closed, and the tourists are all out."

I knew that meant big problems as I rushed to my truck and sped toward Section III. "John, what's your 20?" The term "20" in radio communications refers to location.

"I'm down by the back lakes," he answered.

When I rounded the last corner, I could see the problem. A dead white rhino was floating in the lake. "What the heck is goin' on?" I asked John, who had an equally puzzled look on his face.

"I don't have a clue. We just happened to drive by and noticed it."

"Well, let's get him out of there and see if we can do an autopsy," I suggested.

This would be a first for me. I had been very lucky and not had many autopsies to do since I started working at the park. I certainly had never done one on a white rhino.

All sorts of things were flashing through my mind as they began the process of attaching ropes to the floating rhino to pull him toward shore. My first thought — and greatest worry — was that a disease had felled him and would be contagious to the others. I was hoping for a simple solution that this was an isolated incident where he just slipped, fell into the water, and drowned. Since some of the banks were steep and the lake was deep in places, that actually seemed logical.

They hauled the corpse from the lake, and I immediately began to inspect it. I got a sick feeling inside, seeing such a beautiful animal dead for no apparent reason. It was a young bull, probably four or five years old, and weighed about 2,500 to 2,800 pounds.

As a forklift rolled the body over and over for me, the only marks I found on the huge animal were some deep punctures in the throat area. There had been a lot of sparring and fighting among the male rhinos since the breeding had started last year, so I wrote off the punctures as sparring wounds. Since he was slightly smaller than the others, it made sense that he might have suffered more injuries during the battles. The punctures were not particularly round in nature, but slightly jagged and torn around the edges.

After a very thorough five-hour autopsy, the only other thing I found was a great deal of fluid deep in the lung parenchyma (the connective tissue framework), which appeared to be the result of drowning. Maybe the rhinos were fighting, and the others pushed him into the lake where he drowned. I took a complete set of tissue samples so I could send them off to Texas A&M in order to rule out any infection or contagious disease; nevertheless, there were no apparent signs of disease overall.

This was very puzzling indeed, and I didn't like the fact that I didn't have a complete answer. I advised management what I thought may have happened, and they seemed content with my assessment at that time. All we could do then was wait to see if this was going to be an isolated incident.

Days went by, and during that time all of the tests on the tissue samples came back from the Texas A&M Diagnostic Lab. All results proved negative for any disease, and examination of the lung tissue indicated that the rhino had actually drowned.

For some reason, however, this explanation was still strange to me. It just didn't all fit, but meanwhile all was quiet.

About eight o'clock one morning, a few days after the test results had come back, John Clay came into my office and shut the door. "Doc," he spoke quietly and concerned, "you aren't goin' to believe this, but we have another floater in Section III."

I could feel that sick feeling coming back again. "You are kiddin' me, aren't you?"

"I'm as serious as a heart attack." He wasn't smiling.

"John, what on earth is goin' on?" I asked with grave concern.

"I don't have a clue, and the big thing I don't understand is how they're getting in the lake in the first place. I've already got the section closed, and we're pulling him out."

As I drove toward Section III again, I analyzed my sick feeling. It was more from the sheer frustration of not knowing what was going on than anything else. As I approached the dead rhino, my sickness became mixed with sadness when I saw this second magnificent creature lying there on the bank.

Once again, the first thing I noticed was some jagged puncture wounds in the throat area. This one was a larger female, which would probably not support my initial theory of the animal fighting and being pushed by other rhinos into the lake.

Several hours later my second autopsy was complete and produced the same results: it appeared she had drowned. Just as I finished, I was startled when I turned around and found Bill York standing there. I knew it was only a matter of time before management wanted some answers.

"What the bloody hell is going on here, Doc?" I could tell by his red face that his blood pressure was up, and he was not happy.

"Looks the same as the other one," I replied. "These marks here on the throat are identical to those on other rhino, and the lungs indicate that the cause of death was drowning."

"Healthy rhinos just don't wander into a lake and drown," Bill muttered. "I just don't understand it."

"I'll send these tissues in to A&M also, but I don't expect to find anything in the way of a disease."

"Joe, I know you're doing all you can do to solve this, but this simply can't go on." With that, Bill walked out, jumped into his Jeep, and speed away.

John and I looked at each other, concerned and wondering where to go from there. We had lost two white rhino in less than three weeks and

One of our first rhino calves born in Section III.

we didn't have a clue what was causing their deaths.

"John, let's put an all-day watch on this rhino herd," I said. "I don't care if it takes an extra man or overtime or what. We need some answers!"

"Works for me. I'll start it tomorrow."

Three or four more weeks went by with no

Mother and baby relaxing.

more casualties. During that time we were blessed with our first rhino birth. It was a little male, and he was a ball of fire. The new mother was extremely possessive and would not let anyone, not even another rhino, near her new baby. This happy event took everyone's mind off our unsolved mystery. We managed one more week of bliss before the bottom fell out again.

I knew we were in trouble when John stormed into my office and slammed the door. "Doc, we did what you told us to do, and we babysat that rhino herd every day, and I'll be if we didn't come in this mornin' and find another rhino floatin' in the lake. I guess whatever happened, happened during the night."

My heart sank, and I actually felt nauseated. I just stared at John in disbelief.

"Same marks on the throat?"

"Can't tell yet. We can't get it to shore."

"Why not? What's the holdup?"

"That big hippo who lives in that lake is actually pushing the body around with his nose and seems protective of it."

"John, have you been drinkin'?"

"Not hardly, but my rangers aren't goin' near that rhino as long as that hippo is around."

"OK, put out some grain on the shore and, when the hippo comes out to eat, you can row in and snag the body," I suggested.

When I arrived at the lake, I found that the hippo family was eating contentedly and John and his crew were just then getting the body to shore. If all of this wasn't bad enough, this rhino was another big female but with an enlarged mammary gland.

"John, I hope this isn't goin' to be a pregnant female."

"You and me both."

As I gazed around the section trying to count our remaining females, I suddenly became very worried. I couldn't find our new mother. I could see the baby whirling and running and another rhino trying to run it away from the herd, but there was no mother taking up for the baby. Not a good sign.

I knew the new mother had a split right ear so when they drug the carcass to shore, I asked, "John, does this rhino have a split right ear?"

"Sure does." Knowing what this meant, John slammed his Jeep door in disgust. "That's all we need, Doc. I'm about ready to quit!"

"I know, man. We can't seem to get a break."

I could hear another Jeep in the background and knew that would be Bill. I couldn't even fathom having to tell him we had three dead rhino in six weeks and now an orphan to capture and raise. I decided to let John tell him.

It seemed like forever before we got Bill settled down.

"All right guys, listen up!" Bill hollered in his thick accent. "It's obvious to me that we have a rhino killer in our midst. I'm not sure at this point whether

Mixing up a dart.

it's man or beast, but we *will* find out. I want a 24-hour watch on this rhino herd starting tonight, and I want an answer and I want it soon." Without another word, he slammed the door on his Jeep and tore off down the road.

"Well, John, I guess that leaves the details of the autopsy an' the baby rhino capture to us."

John nodded and then asked, "Ever caught a baby rhino?"

"No, but I bet we can handle that part. The raisin' of it may be a different story."

We had good luck with our cheetah orphans, and there was no reason to think we couldn't raise a strong, frisky rhino calf. The autopsy was like all of the others, and the neck wounds were also the same. It was almost spooky at that point.

I decided to use a very low .05 cc dose of M-99 for the baby rhino, and I knew we had better get him quick before another rhino decided to play Ping-Pong with him. I was able to drive right up to him and managed a well-placed shot in his right shoulder. He began to stagger within a couple of minutes; then, we immediately grabbed him. As we were putting him into a small crate, one of the wardens commented on how smooth and firm he was, like a football. From that point on, his name was "Football."

Somebody said night patrols were slated to start that evening, and since there was nothing more I could do in the park I headed to the nursery to introduce Football to Kay. The wardens had unloaded the crate, and he was waking up when I got there.

"Kay! Kay, where are you? I have a surprise for you!" I yelled, as I peeked around a nursery door.

"Your surprises scare me to death." She had walked up from behind in an attempt to startle me.

"I've got somethin' here for you that kinda fits your personality. It's ornery, tough, an' lovable, all at the same time."

"That's me," she beamed. "What is it?"

"It's over here in this crate and it needs a mother." I pointed to the crate.

"I don't believe this! First, you give me two cheetah cubs, which are endangered, and now a white rhino calf, also endangered. No pressure at all, huh?" But she quickly got down to business by asking, "What kind of milk should I use?"

"We're goin' to try goat's milk diluted down with water. Their butterfat is very close to a rhino's, and I think it will work. Oh, by the way, his name is Football," I volunteered as I walked out of the room. I had all the confidence in the world that Kay could raise the rhino and, as it turned out, I was right. She did the same quality job as she had done with the cheetahs.

Two more weeks passed with no news from Section III. Football was thriving, drinking in the neighborhood of two gallons of milk every day. It was on a Monday morning following a busy weekend when I heard from John again.

"Doc, get down here quick!" he boomed over the radio. I could tell by the excitement in his voice that he had the answer to the rhino saga.

John came running up to my truck as I stopped. "I've got good news and bad news," he declared. "The good news is we know what's killing our rhino, but the bad news is that we watched one more die."

Football enjoying having a tummy rub.

Football and my two sons cautiously checking each other out.

I looked out in the lake, and sure enough there was another dead rhino. This one was fresh, however, and hadn't had time to bloat up and float. Although he was part in and part out of the water, he was very dead, with blood oozing from his neck. Even with all of this, I still couldn't figure out the answer.

"It's Big Daddy," John said sadly.

"What are you talkin' about? A hippo can't kill a rhino."

"Well, Jason watched him do it. He told me that, when the rhino walked to the lake's edge to drink, he saw a huge mouth open up and spring from the water, grabbin' the rhino by the throat. Big Daddy used his heavier weight to pull the rhino down the bank and under the water. The rhino was dead in a matter of minutes. Jason saw the whole thing, Doc."

I was in shock, but this made sense. It explained the puncture wounds on the neck; still, it was mind-boggling. I had heard and read reports of large hippo killing and eating cattle, small antelope, and even natives in Africa — but a one-and-a-half-ton rhino? Unbelievable!

Big Daddy was appropriately named, weighing more than 5,000 pounds. He was considered aggressive, but why would he do it? Was it territorial, or just for the pleasure of killing? My gut feeling was that it was territorial. If he felt a rhino was intruding into his territory when it came to drink at a specific part of the lake, then he might act accordingly. I figured we probably would never know the reason with absolute certainty, but we were content that we had our killer.

The next question was what to do about it? I knew how Mr. York would probably solve the problem when he learned about Big Daddy.

"Doc, Bill's on his way down and he's not happy about losing another rhino," John whispered.

When Bill stepped out of his Jeep, he was carrying his .458-caliber Special. "Where's that killer hippo?" he shouted.

"He's in the lake," John answered. "We haven't seen him surface in a while."

"Well, when he does, I have a surprise for him."

I could see Bill's logic, but I was desperately looking for an alternate plan. From Bill's point of view, Big Daddy had already cost us four rhino. He would be impossible to capture for relocation, and we didn't have a place to relocate him anyway. We couldn't move all the rhino from this beautiful section because they were breeding and thriving. The irony of it all was that we had achieved an environment so natural that we were experiencing behavior just as we might in the wild.

Bill, being born in South Africa, was going to handle the situation just as they would have in the wild. When you have a rogue animal upsetting the ecological balance of nature, you simply take him out.

There had to be a better solution; but, even if there was one, convincing Bill of any other option at that point might be a chore in itself. As I scrambled different scenarios over in my mind, I kept remembering those giant canine teeth I saw on those occasions when Big Daddy yawned. They were the reason for those jagged, deep punctures on the victims' necks. It occurred to me that, without those canines, Big Daddy would be disarmed and unable to grasp his prey. I knew time was running out so I quickly ran over to Bill.

"Bill, I've got a suggestion for a possible alternative solution to Big Daddy."

Big Daddy showing off his teeth.

"I already have the solution here in my hand, Doc, and when he surfaces again I'll solve this problem."

Suddenly I remembered my younger days in Dublin, when I was arguing with my dad when he was dead set on shooting Silky. This time, however, I was no longer a young boy, but I was again trying to use reason with another angry, grown man to save an animal's life. To me, the principles were still the same.

"Bill, if I can get those canine teeth out, he will be virtually disarmed and harmless. He would still be a magnificent exhibit animal for the park."

"Joe, immobilizing a hippo is not an exact science. He would probably drown anyway since they always run into the water when they're darted or startled."

"At least there's a chance," I pleaded. "And if it works, we can write it up in the AAZPA (American Association of Zoological Parks and Aquariums) journal, and you can co-author." I was trying anything.

"How would you extract those giant teeth even if you could immobilize him on land?"

"I'll figure that out. I've got some special saws and instruments that I think will work."

"Oh, what the heck, Joe, go ahead and try it," Bill relented. "It does beat the alternative. Let's get it done today. Let me know when you're planning it, and we'll get it on film."

I could see the PR wheels turning in Bill's head, but at least we had an alternate plan.

I told John that Big Daddy had narrowly escaped certain death, and he looked pleased. I asked him to get a large forklift, lots of heavy-duty nylon rope, and some special sweet feed that Big Daddy loved. I then drove to my clinic to get the proper tools I would need for the job. I decided to use Gigli wire to saw the teeth at the base if I couldn't dig them out by the roots.

In two hours we both were ready to go and were promptly joined by Bill and a film crew. I loaded a dart with 5 cc of M-99 and 1 cc Rompun. I hoped that the second drug would stop the roaming and prancing phase of the narcotic M-99, and that Big Daddy would just keep eating after he was hit and lie down on land, rather than run for the water when he was darted.

We placed a huge pile of sweet feed at Big Daddy's favorite feeding spot and waited. Sure enough, in about 15 minutes, here he came. He surfaced, looked at the pile, sniffed, and then made a beeline toward it. As I watched him chomp the grain, I could see his huge canines more closely, and I could more easily understand how he could grab his prey and use his superior weight and leverage to drag a rhino to its death.

When the dart hit him, he did exactly what Bill had projected. He hit the water with such force that he created a small wake on the lake, and then he quickly submerged like a submarine making a final dive.

I looked at Bill and said, "You were right, but it was worth a try. At least we didn't invite the news media. You can shoot him later."

As we were loading our equipment — having given up — the most amazing thing happened. That monstrous beast surfaced near the feed, walked out on land, and collapsed right next to it. It was as if he wasn't going to let a sting in his rear stop him from having lunch. Bill and I looked at each other and smiled.

"We may get to write that paper for the AAZVA journal yet, Doc," Bill said with a degree of excitement in his voice. "Now all you have to do is get those teeth out and then reverse him, so when he goes back into the water he's completely awake."

We knew we didn't have much time. While John set up our portable anesthetic machine, I grabbed my tools and went to work. We used two large cotton ropes and a hoist to hold the giant jaws open, which provided me with good access. Up close the teeth were much larger and thicker than I imagined; I knew that trying to remove them by their roots was futile.

I immediately started sawing at the gum line with the Gigli wire. The wire saw is made primarily for cutting bones, so sawing through the hard enamel was a long task, taking about an hour of start-and-stop sawing. One tooth, after it was removed, measured more than 14 inches in length and was about 6 inches in diameter. I still have the teeth to this day, and they are some of my most treasured possessions. After I finished I administered the M-50-50 reversal IV through a leg vein and some Yohimbine, which produces cardiovascular effects including increases in heart rate and blood pressure. The M-50-50 reversed the M-

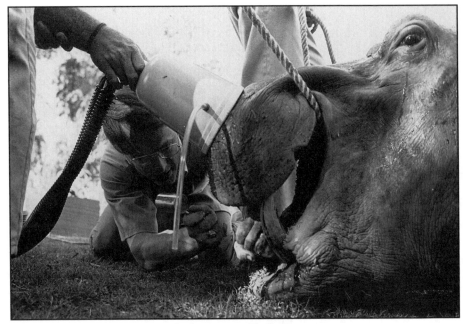

Oral surgery on Big Daddy.

99, and the Yohimbine reversed the effects of Rompun. We removed the gas anesthetic mask from his nostrils and waited. After what felt like an eternity, Big Daddy simply stood up and started eating again. The entire process had actually worked.

Bill and I both were elated. Not only had we solved our rhino problem, we had managed to save another one of Mother Nature's own.

Looking back and trying to analyze the reason for the rhino deaths, I still believe it was a territorial thing. Yes, hippos do occasionally kill or mutilate natives who are in or near the water, and they have been seen eating small antelope that ventured too close to the water's edge. The aggression is about food or protection of territory. Once we had Big Daddy disarmed, we never lost another rhino. We did have several baby hippo born in Section III, which I'm sure were a direct result of Big Daddy's efforts. Isn't it great how Mother Nature balances it all out?

With this rhino episode behind me, I was able to spend some quality time with my family and enjoy playing with the cheetah cubs and Football. My sons Chad and Troy, now at ages eight and four, were fascinated by Football but were not confident enough to touch him. They thought it was great fun to watch from a distance as I scratched and rubbed him. Playing with the cubs and Football provided me with many hours of enjoyment and happiness, and having the opportunity to watch them grow into maturity was one of the most rewarding experiences of my life.

Just being a small part of wildlife survival was very special, and I will always look back on these days with pride.

Second rhino calf born in Section III.

Big Daddy and one of his cows at home in the swampy area of Secion III.

CHAPTER 10

JUDY, JUDY, JUDY

I can honestly say that I have never been a great primate lover, and perhaps that's because of their strength and unpredictability. I also felt intimidated by their intelligence, which would explain my lack of enthusiasm when George Gray arrived at my office one day and happily announced that he was bringing an animal movie star to retire and live at the wildlife park.

I had never met George but had heard a lot about him. He was well respected for his animal knowledge, which accounted for the fact that he was in charge of any movie work, such as commercials and public events involving the animals. I didn't know if the animals were afraid of him or respected him but, in any event, I had heard that George always got the job done.

"Dr. Cannon, where are you?" came a booming voice from down the hall. When I looked out my door and down the hallway, I couldn't believe my eyes. There I saw a very large, hulk of a man with red hair, red complexion, and a very serious expression on his face. He came walking down the hall leading a full-grown chimpanzee by the hand.

"Doc, got someone that wants to meet you," George chuckled. "George Gray here," the big man announced as he stuck out his hand, "and this is my girlfriend, Judy."

I had just finished shaking George's hand when Judy stuck out her hand, too. My heart skipped a beat, and I could feel a knot in my stomach as I thought, *What do I do now?* To let her or George know that I was not fond of primates could be a catastrophe for a wild animal veterinarian. Instinct, however, overpowered me, and I slowly offered my hand to Judy. Instead of jerking my arm off, as I feared a 110-pound chimp might do, she merely shook it lightly three or four times and raised her upper lip in a chimp smile.

"I think she likes you." George smiled, and then added, "She usually doesn't like strangers."

"Well, that's good, I guess," I said with some relief as I swallowed hard. "George, I've heard a lot about you from Bill York. Bill says you're the best in the business."

George laughed. "I'm probably one of a few people around crazy enough to even attempt to work wild animals on a movie set with a lot of nutty people around. Take Judy here; she was a pleasure to work with and is as smart as they come, Doc. She was the original chimp on the TV series, *Daktari*, which was aired back in the 1960s."

George turned to Judy and barked, "Smile for the good doctor, Judy." With that command she peeled back her top and bottom lips. As I watched carefully, I couldn't help but notice that she was missing her incisors and canine teeth.

"What happened to her teeth?" I asked George. "Can she eat with all of those teeth missing?"

"Like us, a chimp chews with their jaw teeth, so on that count she is fine. I'm not sure what happened to her teeth. I know she lost many of her teeth when she was young and I reckon her age has taken care of the rest. She can still be dangerous, Doc, so always be careful around her or any other chimp."

"Has she ever hurt anyone to your knowledge?"

"A couple of years ago, she began to get a little cranky and even attacked a couple of girls on the set while they were shooting some commercials. They retired her from *Daktari* after that. That is where I came in. Our job is to make Judy comfortable here and allow her to live her life out in peace. She has been through a lot. When man tries to train an animal and impose his will on it, sometimes it doesn't work and it's not really fair to the animal. Judy is only about 26 years old and still has a lot of good years left, since chimps can live to be around 40 years. She's used to me so I'll be the only one handling her here at this park. We will probably shoot a few TV commercials with her now and then, but that's all, so there won't be nearly as much stress for her."

My morning was getting more interesting by the minute. I had no idea I would meet a movie star and her trainer. All of the time George was talking to me, Judy had been staring intently at me. I was getting very uncomfortable, especially with all of the background information George had given me. All of a sudden, as quickly as she had shaken my hand, she hopped up in my arms, locked her legs around my waist, put her arms around my neck and gave me a big, wet kiss with her tongue.

I was petrified! I have seldom been that scared, and it all happened so fast that George couldn't believe his eyes. Then, just as quickly as she had kissed me, she hopped back over to George, gave her hand back to him, and began making short, contented chirps.

"Well, that's the darnedest thing I've ever seen in my life!" George exclaimed. "She's never done that with anyone, and I've known her for over 15 years."

I was still shaking. I just didn't like or trust primates and, lo and behold, I had just been kissed by one. Finally I got enough strength back to speak. "What do you make of that?"

"Love at first sight, that's the only answer," George chuckled.

"Well, I ain't havin' no affair with no used up, psycho, ex-*Daktari* monkey," I joked.

"You better watch what you say. Sometimes I think she can understand us," the big man said before he and Judy wheeled and walked back down the hallway.

"Kissed by a monkey," I muttered to myself. I kept spitting to get any monkey germs out of my mouth.

A couple of days later I saw George and Judy again. As I was walking by the River Ride in the amusement park area, I noticed George and Judy sharing a Dr Pepper in front of a movie camera with no operator behind it. Judy was wearing sunglasses and sitting with her legs crossed in a lawn chair. Judy would take a sip of Dr Pepper, hand it to George, and he would take a sip.

I couldn't believe my eyes. I had no idea she was so talented. When Judy saw me, she immediately ran to me with the Dr Pepper and handed it to me. *If I don't drink some of it, she'll get mad; and if I do, I'll surely die of some exotic monkey disease like B-virus or hepatitis.*

I had to do something, so I acted like I took a sip and then handed it back to her. She took a sip and handed it back to me again. By that time George had arrived to collect his star and chuckled. "Your new girlfriend brought you a Dr Pepper and, believe me, you did the right thing to drink it."

"I didn't think I had a choice, George," I confessed. "Just tryin' to please."

George looked puzzled. "I don't know why she's chosen you as her new best friend, but she has and believe me, she's usually not like that."

George took her by the hand, saying, "Come on, Judy, it's back to our Dr Pepper commercial. We're on the clock." With that, he guided her back to the set.

It was about a week later before I saw Judy again; she and George were riding around in George's truck. And no, Judy was not driving. I stopped my vet truck along side George and rolled down my window. As soon as Judy recognized me, she started jumping up and down, screaming and chirping.

"Wave at her, Doc." George ordered.

I waved at her with my right hand, and she waved back with her right hand. I waved at her with my left hand, and she waved back with her left hand.

"She's missed you, can't you see?" George laughed again.

At that point she politely opened the passenger door, got out, and came over to my vet truck; then, she opened the door on the passenger side, got in, and made herself at home.

"Well, you've done it now, Doc. You've picked yourself up a lady hitchhiker and you might as well go ahead and give her a tour of the park. She's not going to be happy until you do."

Acting on George's request, I slowly drove away. I figured George never would have advised me to do so if he hadn't felt I was safe. As we drove around, Judy just sat there looking at me or looking out the window. She seemed a little bored, and since I didn't know what to do and George wasn't around, I offered her some of the gum I was chewing. She took it, rolled it around with her fingers into a perfect ball, popped it into her mouth, and swallowed it. Oops, bad idea. Now what?

Since I was afraid to stop for fear of getting mauled, I just kept driving. It seemed like the more she saw, the less bored and happier she became. I drove her all over the parking lot area and around the River Ride section. Naturally, I saw everyone that even remotely knew me, and I guess it was this tour that started all the talk.

Almost everyone I came in contact with the next few days wanted to know about my new "girlfriend." Even before that day, the news had spread about how much Judy liked me, so this was the final proof the staff needed in order to tease me unmercifully.

"Hey, Doc, saw you had a date with your new girlfriend," Ray Sutton chided as he walked by my office door days later. Ray was a new warden who had moved down from Michigan; even he had begun kidding me about Judy. This thing had grown out of hand, but oh well, I had decided to make the best of it.

Over the next few months, I grew more attached to her and more relaxed around her. No matter where Judy saw me, she would stop whatever she was doing, run right to me, and show her affection. Occasionally, when she was through with her morning TV shoots, I would pick her up in my truck and bring her back to the lab to hang around the nursery while I did my routine treatments and surgeries. She would sit in my chair and watch everything I did. When I would draw up shots to give injections, she would cover her eyes and squeal, showing her displeasure for needles.

I could tell her to bring me a Dr Pepper, and she would go down the hall to the refrigerator, open the door, and bring one back. Of course, I had to share it with her. I figured if I had some exotic monkey disease, it was too late anyway so it didn't make any difference if I drank after her. This sharing of our Dr Pepper, sip by sip, was a bonding thing, and Judy really liked it. I had read about the intelligence of primates but until becoming deeply involved with one, I had no idea as to their I.Q. and emotions. It was almost scary.

Along about that time, I had grown so comfortable with Judy that I felt I was ready to introduce her to my family. She seemed harmless enough, and I knew that if my children could experience even a fraction of the enjoyment that I had, it would be a fantastic experience for them. I had been telling my two sons about her for some time, and they couldn't wait to meet her. I expected them to be somewhat intimidated when they came face to face with her.

I chose the later part of October for the introduction. It was getting close to Halloween, and the park had a lot of trick-or-treat publicity planned for Judy. Judy and another monkey friend named Bo were scheduled to be in the front part of Section I handing out Halloween candy, so this was my chance. The boys could meet her and get some candy to boot.

As I pulled my family's white Suburban into the line to meet Judy and Bo, I was curious how Judy would react to seeing me with my children and not in my vet truck. Judy and Bo were kept in pretty close tow for liability reasons and were not allowed to approach the cars unless they were with a handler.

Well, when Judy saw me, she started jumping up and down, grabbed Bo by the hand, and both chimps walked straight to our car, offering us candy with no handler around. As startled as the handlers were, it didn't stop Fred Coston from capturing some good video of his chimps roaming free as they handed out Halloween candy.

Judy and Bo handing out candy to Chad and Troy in Section I.

My sons were ecstatic and they, too, began jumping up and down with excitement. I half expected Judy to come and get into the car with us, but she just stood there looking longingly at me as if to say, "I'm working now, but pick me up later when I'm off."

When I got back to the office after taking my family home, I was greeted by Fred: "Doc, that was great out there and so natural. I can't believe those two chimps were so docile and got along with you so well."

"Just my magnetic personality," I joked.

"Well, whatever it is, I'd sure like to get some more pictures of the chimps and your boys, if you don't mind."

117

"Let's go get some candy."

"What do you have in mind?"

"Maybe dressing up the boys and the chimps in trick-or-treat costumes. What do you think?"

"As long as the handlers are close by, I guess it will be all right."

"You bet. I can make that happen. When can you get back out with the boys?"

"Halloween is tomorrow night so I could bring them tomorrow afternoon in their costumes before we take them trick-or-treating."

"Great! See you at four o'clock tomorrow?"

"That'll work." As I walked out of the office I had an uneasy feeling, but I figured as long as Judy had a handler that it would be OK. Chad and Troy could hardly sleep that night in anticipation of their Halloween dates.

I had to admit that, as I watched the photographs being taken the following day, I was in total awe. There stood Judy in her Tweety Bird shirt, Bo in his Space Witch costume, Chad dressed as King Kong, and Troy costumed as Spiderman. It almost was as if there was no missing link between primates and man. They all looked happy and ready to go trick-or-treating. After several still and video shots, the boys and I got into the Suburban to continue our Halloween trek, while Judy and Bo went back into Section I to keep handing out candy.

Weeks passed, and I was spending more and more time with Judy. People still were talking, all in jest, of course. But we did enjoy each other's company and had definitely connected.

One day — when I got real brave or real stupid — I drove Judy over to my house, unescorted by her trainer or a handler. A lot of the time she and I had spent together was unmonitored, and I figured this would fall into that category. After all, she had been around my kids, and they had gotten along fine.

I called ahead to tell the boys to set up a table and chairs on the back porch because we were going to have a surprise guest. As I pulled up to the back of the house with Judy, Chad and Troy came running up to the truck yelling, "Judy, Judy, Judy," again jumping up and down with excitement.

I cautioned them to slow down, not to yell or scream around her, and just to go sit down at the table. I asked them to get Judy a Dr Pepper from the refrigerator inside, and when they were seated at the table, I would bring Judy over to them.

Judy was equally excited to see the boys, and I think she sensed that they were my sons. Once they calmed down, she also became calm, politely sitting at the table. She was very slow and deliberate around them and made no aggressive moves at all. Judy was usually very obedient and would not reach for or do anything unless she was told to do so. She looked longingly at the can of Dr Pepper sitting on the table but she wouldn't dare reach for it.

By that time I had decided it was time to quench our thirst. "Chad, could you please open the Dr Pepper and take the first sip and then hand it to Judy?" He looked at me like I had lost my mind but did it anyway. Judy gently took the drink from him and guzzled about a fourth of the can before handing it back to Chad. By then the boys were beside themselves, giggling so hard they could barely sit in their chairs.

"OK, Chad, take a drink and give it back." I coaxed.

"No way, Dad, I'm not drinking after her."

"Well, then give it to Troy and let him drink."

Troy took it, acted like he was drinking and then handed the drink to me. Since I had done this numerous times and had yet to contract some deadly disease, I took the drink and guzzled a fourth of the can. After a couple of more guzzles, Judy and I had finished the drink.

"Crush the can, Judy," I urged.

She immediately took the can, put it between her two palms, and proceeded to make a can pancake. That was the final straw! The boys literally were laughing so hard they were on the edges of their chairs.

Judy seemed to be a little restless so I figured we had better quit while we were ahead. I told the boys goodbye and told Judy to wave bye to them. Judy waved all the way to the truck and continued while we were driving away.

This couldn't have been a better afternoon and one that I would always remember and cherish. It was hard to know how Chad and Troy perceived this interaction between man and animal, but I hoped they would have the same good memories of their childhood days as I did. I hoped that in some way this had helped to give them a better understanding of God's creatures.

I didn't trust Judy around Amy, my daughter, since Judy had a history over the years of not relating well to females. I sure didn't want to take a chance. Amy had helped me out in the nursery on occasion, and enjoyed interacting with animals such as baby zebra, baby ostrich, and several lion cubs. Amy was gentle with the nursery animals and got along with them well. She had no fear of them and, in a way, that was good, as I think most animals can sense that fear. Her love for animals continued into adulthood; again, I hoped that in some small way these experiences gave her a deeper understanding of animals.

The following summer, on a hot July day, I was making my rounds, trying to get as much accomplished as I could in one day. Things were going great at the park, but I hadn't seen Judy in a couple of weeks because I had just been too busy.

She was the furthest thing from my mind as I rounded the corner by the cafeteria, heading to the train ride section to treat a sick wallaby. I caught a glimpse of a group of people out of the corner of my eye and slowed down to see who they were. It was George Gray and some people I didn't recognize; they had their attention focused on something out in the lake. These smaller lakes were only about four feet deep and were used for paddleboat rides for the kids.

I wonder what they're lookin' at? I walked to the water's edge. There, to my surprise, was Judy dressed up in a hula skirt, sunglasses, and a funny little hat. If that wasn't enough, they had her floating around in a little raft, and Judy didn't look happy.

When Judy spotted me, she was just as surprised to see me as I was to see her. The cameras were rolling, and it was obvious they were shooting a commercial. Big George spotted me about the same time Judy did, halted the cameras, and started pulling her raft toward shore. I guessed that he figured her concentration would be gone anyway since she had seen me. I also noticed that — as the big man pulled Judy's raft to shore — he was about as flushed as a fair complexioned, red-haired person could get. I couldn't tell if that was from the sun or just the exertion of pulling Judy to shore. While listening to the cameramen talk, however, it became obvious that they were shooting some type of suntan lotion commercial and that Judy was the star of the day.

George was angry as he barked orders to all of the people around the water's edge. "Get back!" he yelled. "Give us room. We've got an angry chimp here." George was out of breath, very red faced, and obviously losing his patience. "Get back! Get back! We've got work to do here. Give us room."

I just stood there, not knowing exactly what to do. I had unintentionally interrupted a TV shoot and I was feeling responsible since Judy had stopped co-operating the instant she saw me.

"I'm sorry, George, I had no idea what was goin' on or who was over here, or I would have never interrupted you."

"Don't worry, Doc, we were quitting anyway." George kept reeling Judy in towards the bank and yelling to everyone. "Get back, I tell you! We've got an upset chimp here."

I noticed that Judy had begun to squirm nervously in her raft and I could see that her genital area was swollen, indicating that she was currently in her estrous cycle. All of this was starting to build as Judy arrived at the shore. I had moved back with the rest of the crowd to give George some room and thought I had conveniently hidden in the crowd.

Not so. Judy got out of the boat and, instead of grabbing George's hand, bolted straight for me. I just froze. I already felt partially responsible for this fiasco and really didn't know what to do. Judy came bounding right up to me, jumped into my arms, putting her feet around my waist and her arms around my neck like she always did. She did seem upset, but I took the whole thing as if she was trying to tell me, "Take me away from all of this."

She was just about ready to give me a big kiss and settle into my arms when Big George entered stage right. He was huffing and puffing after his short run up the hill and he looked madder than ever.

"Let me have her, Doc. She's not herself today," he said as he reached out to Judy. She reluctantly gave him her hand. I just held my ground and stood still, and the instant that Judy gave George her hand he literally yanked her from me with all of the force that a 400-pound man can muster. George meant well and was only trying to protect me, but it didn't turn out that way.

Then it happened! She jerked away from George and the next thing I knew I saw a screeching, screaming Judy with her hair bristled along her back, heading straight for me. This time, however, she was even madder. Not totally sure of her intentions, I just froze again and hoped I could calm her down. I had no reason to be afraid of her because we were "buds."

Judy never slowed down. She didn't jump into my arms. She went straight for my left leg and proceeded to force about half of my thigh into the back portion of her mouth where her remaining teeth were. She did this by using her hands and fingers to push my leg from behind. I could feel her fingernails and then her teeth and jaw pressure crunching into the top part of my thigh. She literally had a death grip on my thigh and had no intention of letting it go.

I was in shock and disbelief, and was starting to be in pain. I kept waiting — and hoping — for her to release my thigh, but she continued to hold her grip. The next sensation I felt was blood starting to run down my leg and into my boot. This had gotten out of hand. Was I just going to stand there and let her destroy my leg or was I going to defend myself?

I looked around for some help and to my amazement found the crowd had dwindled to only a handful of stragglers and Big George. The remaining people just suddenly turned and ran, and although Big George tried, he wasn't able to help much either. Imagine a mad, fat man kicking a chimp that was attached to my leg and jumping at every kick. Each time he would kick, he would get red-faced and almost fall down. One thing was for sure: Judy had no intentions of releasing her grip.

The situation was deteriorating rapidly. It had begun to look like it was going to be up to Judy and myself to sort this thing out. I just couldn't get over the shock that my friend was trying to kill me, but as the blood continued to fill my boot, the pain had grown almost unbearable. It became alarmingly clear that she meant business. My emotions had changed from shock and disbelief to anger, and I could feel my instincts to fight for survival swelling inside of me.

As I glanced down at that thick dark head, only to see it still attached to my thigh, I realized that our love affair was over and that if I could have found a gun I would most certainly have shot her. With no gun in sight, however, I turned to the old, bar room brawl art of fist-a-cuffs to defend myself. With my right hand I began hitting her in the top of the head with all of my strength. A chimp's skull is about three inches thick over their eyebrows and that's where all of my blows were landing. With every blow she would scream and shake her head in an attempt to tear my leg apart, but she did not let go. After I struck her with a series of right and left hooks to the ears, she finally released her grip and looked up at me.

Now I was the attacker, but as my right hook headed for her jaw, she simply grabbed my hand in midair and proceeded to stick my entire fist into her mouth. Her grip was like an iron vice. Even though I had heard that a chimp has the strength of 10 men, I had never had a personal experience to prove that, not until then.

Try as I might, I couldn't even come close to pulling away from her death grip. With my thigh still bleeding and throbbing, I found I had a new problem. Judy was biting down with all of her might on my right hand. I could hear the bones crunching and feel the sensation of blood pouring from my hand into her mouth. I was starting to feel scared and was getting a little weak in the knees. I was sure I hadn't lost that much blood, but the pain alone was tremendous and was causing me to start to tremble. With my left hand and right leg still working, I continued to fight with all I had. I hit her time after time in the face and even got in a few good kicks.

Still, as I grew weaker, my swings got slower, and then Judy did a surprising thing. She released my right hand and retreated toward the lake, a distance of about 30 feet. This gave me a moment to evaluate my right hand, and it wasn't a pretty sight. I could see that the bone and knuckle were exposed and that a jagged cut was bleeding profusely. I couldn't move my thumb or index finger; this scared me. I couldn't stand on my left leg; that scared me, too.

I thought the ordeal was over and was trying to catch my breath, but then I saw her charging me again — screaming and shrieking — with hair bristling. She was doing her "chimp scramble" and was heading straight for me.

Where's George? Where's anybody? Somebody help me! I braced myself to face my attacker. Since I couldn't run, I was greeted this time by an old wrestling move, a running flying mare. She became airborne about two yards from me and hit me right in the chest with both feet. As her feet made contact, she pushed off and sent me flying to the ground. I could see that she was coming again when I hit the ground, so I quickly sat up, using my good arm to scoot backward and kicked her with all of my might with my good, right leg.

After a couple of kicks to her thick head, she did the old iron chimp thing and grabbed my right leg in midair. Guess what? She stuck my foot into her mouth. As bad as it already was, it was worsened by the fact that I had on a pair of brand new cowboy boots that had cost me more than $300. They were about to be ruined and they were supposed to be the toughest skin available. No one told Judy that, however, and she bit completely through the toe of the boot and into my foot.

Now what? My left leg was numb and bleeding, my right hand was mangled and bleeding, and at that point my right foot was useless and bleeding inside Judy's mouth. I screamed, "Is anybody goin' to get this monkey off me?" Same response: no answer.

After what seemed like an eternity, she finally released my right foot and retreated back toward the lake. Somehow I managed to struggle up on my feet, only to realize I could barely stand. I tried to catch my breath and I actually remember seeing God's face and my mother's; I was hallucinating for sure. I was weak, near shock, exhausted, and could barely breathe.

Judy waited a good 30 seconds before her next assault, which gave me a chance to at least clear some of the cobwebs. She may have been taking a short breather herself, but for whatever reason she soon came back again. I tried to brace myself just before she became airborne with the same old flying mare, kicking off with her back feet. I fell again, only this time onto concrete. She had kicked me onto the sidewalk that surrounded the lake.

Since I had no appendages that were working, I decided to roll over on my stomach and play dead. Wrong decision! She immediately grabbed my ears with her hands and proceeded to beat my face and teeth into the concrete. I guessed that the ultimate rejection was worse than confrontation, but I had no choice. As I lay there and felt my face being altered, I was certain that it was over for me. I did manage a couple of strong jerks, however, and with that she again released me and retreated.

I refuse to just lay here and die. Somehow I was able to struggle back to my feet. I stood up just in time to be greeted with my third flying mare. Within seconds Judy was doing a tap dance and drum roll on my chest while screaming at the top of her lungs.

Oh, what the heck, I might as well throw my last good hand at her. Again, I weakly let my left fist fly, but she responded in the same familiar manner. She grabbed my hand in midair and stuck it in her mouth up to my wrist. She bit right through my watch, which was the last gift my mother had given me not long before she died. When Judy was through demolishing my watch and wrist, she grabbed me by an arm and a leg and spun me around a couple of times. I thought I was dead, and I blacked out.

When I regained consciousness, I could hear the sound of people talking. I opened my eyes and saw Big George. He had resurfaced, had Judy by the hand, and was heading back to his truck. I couldn't believe it. I was alive!

My stay in the Arlington Memorial Hospital was somewhat longer than previous visits since they had to do a great deal of detail work on my hand, wrist, leg, foot, and face. I even required a few visits to the dentist to fix my bent and broken teeth. I was lucky. Again, God had spared me.

Looking back on the whole ordeal, I blamed myself more than anybody or anything because, for the third or fourth time, I got too comfortable around an animal. I forgot that she, like the others, was a wild and intelligent animal with feelings and emotions that cannot always be kept under control. In short, I got careless.

After that incident, the park policy changed and handlers were allowed less and less contact with the primates. Park management decided that the training and handling of exotic animals was not such a good idea. There was an exception, of course, to provide for orphaned animals that needed a temporary human caregiver. The revised policy was not just because of the danger to humans, but we had all begun to realize it was too unnatural to impose our way of life on animals that have their own ways. By the late 1980s and early 1990s, most zoos and parks had come to the same realization.

Judy managed to live several more comfortable years at the park, prior to dying of complications from pneumonia. Even though I eventually forgave Judy, our relationship was never the same. Yet, more painful than the agony of my injuries was the sadness that came later as I was picking up my watch, piece by piece, in the sand about 25 yards from the scene of the attack, in the realization that this gift from my mother could never be repaired or replaced.

To this day, some 25 years later, I am constantly reminded of my carelessness by several, large scars on my body and by the two front teeth that are a little crooked and on the uneven side. But that's a good thing. They remind me to be careful and to think before I act.

Tex Case taking Judy back to her island home.

CHAPTER 11

DON'T GET OUT OF THE CAR

The years had passed by quickly at the wildlife park, and surprisingly enough I was still alive and well. No matter how badly an animal had hurt me over the years it was almost always my fault for not giving them enough credit for their intelligence and cunning. I hoped I had learned some lessons and, by exercising caution, could enjoy the rest of my tenure at the park.

My days were filled with routine activities such as vaccinating, hoof trimming, deworming, and caring for any wound or cut that might occur. All of these procedures required chemical immobilization, so I continued to get a lot of practice in the use of the capture gun and M-99. I especially enjoyed being close to the animals, where I could see so much progress in our overall management and breeding program. Almost every species was reproducing and flourishing, which was a result of proper environment and effective herd health programs. It felt great to be a part of the wildlife park and to see the drive-through concept actually working from the game management aspect. I even had more time for my family and friends, so life was good.

The days were almost too calm, but then along came crazy Sam Higgins. Sam had a way of stirring up things. It seemed harmless enough to me when he called and asked if he and his wife Becky could come to the park to take photographs to use on their Christmas cards. They always had very unique Christmas cards; I couldn't even imagine what they had in mind for that year's card.

The previous year, dressed up as Santa Claus, Sam was pictured sitting on a commode with his red pants down around his knees. The caption read, "I'm so happy I could just …!" You can imagine the rest.

Sam definitely was a hoot, and came by the name Crazy Sam very honestly. He was the author of a really good cookbook, *I'm Glad I Ate When I Did, 'Cause I'm Not Hungry Now.* Sam had many talents. With his handle bar mustache and mischievous eyes, he was trouble looking for a place to happen.

I hadn't seen Sam and Becky in a while and was actually looking forward to their visit. I couldn't wait to see what their latest Christmas theme was going to be. I asked him on the phone and he replied, "You'll see soon enough. It's a surprise!" So when Sam, Becky, and their son, Little Sam, showed up dressed as Tarzan, Jane, and Boy, I was not totally surprised. Their costumes were very authentic, right down to the leopard-skin suits. They were quite a sight.

"I'm afraid to even ask what you need from me to complete this year's card," I admitted with a grin.

"Aw, Doc, this year's going to be easy," blurted Sam. "All we need is a

Tarzan and Jane in petting zoo area prior to their "safari."

129

full grown elephant to ride and we'll be set."

"Let me get this straight. You, Becky, and Little Sam want to pose on the back of an elephant for your Christmas card photo?"

"That's right. What do you think?"

"I think you've lost your mind, as usual," I said, smiling.

"Aw, come on, Doc, you and I are pals. You can do it. You don't mean to tell me we got into these outfits for nothin'."

I couldn't believe his guilt trip was working on me and that I was actually thinking of figuring out a way to make this Christmas card thing happen. We did have an adult, Indian elephant named Bubbles, which we sometimes used on rides in the summer. She hadn't been ridden in a while, but she was a good-natured elephant and used to having strangers on her back. I suggested using Bubbles and, of course, that suited Sam fine: anything for the Christmas card.

I explained the risks, but he still didn't have a problem with Bubbles. So, with many reservations on my part, we still proceeded with the plan.

Our elephant man, Armey, brought Bubbles to us and put her through her paces for a while to see how she reacted. She looked fine, and I even got on her to make sure that she was OK. She actually would kneel down

Warming up Bubbles for Tarzan and Jane.

and allow her riders to climb aboard. We normally used a saddle, but Sam wanted the natural look so we went bareback. Actually, everything went as smooth as silk, and everyone was happy. It felt good to help an old friend.

Sam was very appreciative, and I hoped he would quit while we were ahead. But as Sam and Becky were leaving, they asked if they could come out some evening to go on a picture-taking safari at dusk. They wanted to bring out another couple, Dr. Scotty Word and his wife Vivian. Since we all were friends with the other couple, I found it difficult to refuse.

Anyway, what could go wrong on a picture-taking safari in Section I? I asked myself as I mulled over my answer. "What evening are you thinkin' of, Sam?"

"How about this evening? We're already dressed for the occasion, so we might as well go on one."

"That's kinda short notice, Sam, but I guess we can make that work," I agreed reluctantly. "What time do you want to come out?"

"Aw, we'll go by and pick up Scotty and Viv and be out about 5:30 if that's all right."

"Now Sam, I can let you into Section I and Section I only, and there will be strict guidelines on how this deal will work. I really should be with all of you, but I have someplace to be at that time. Just be out here at 5:30, and I'll go over everything with you."

"Doc, don't you worry about us. After all, me Tarzan, she Jane." Sam laughed and seemed very proud of the one-liner he had just come up with out of the clear blue.

I could see the mischievousness in his eyes as he laughed, and at that point I should have known better. For the next few hours I asked myself repeatedly, *What could go wrong in Section I?*

The logical answer kept coming back into my mind: *There are giraffe, wildebeest, eland, blackbuck, antelope, zebra, and other hoof stock out there; and even though they're all wild, they probably won't even come up to their car.* The entire scenario was probably harmless, even if Crazy Sam was involved.

At about 5:30, Sam, Becky, Scotty, and Vivian showed up in Sam's van. Sure enough, Sam still was dressed in his pith helmet and Tarzan outfit, and Becky, of course, was still "Jane." Luckily, they had dropped off "Boy" at the house. Sam was driving and Scotty was sitting on the passenger side, with Becky and Vivian in the back. Scotty had brought his Nikon, the girls had their cameras, and they all were ready for action.

Sam announced that he was just the tour guide and designated driver. I looked in the van for a cooler, which would indicate beer, but didn't see one. They probably had it hidden, though I told Sam earlier that there could be absolutely no drinking under any circumstances. Everything seemed on the up-and-up as we proceeded out to the main gate, which led into Section I. The gates were closed and the guard already had gone home, so I left a ranger posted at the front gate to make sure they would get out safely.

Once inside Section I, I actually climbed into the van through the side door to state the rules for their safari. I explained to them how it would be my rear if anything happened and they didn't follow my exact instructions.

"OK, here are the rules. There are no — and I mean no — exceptions," I said, looking mainly at the girls since I figured they would at least try to make their husbands behave. "Number one: You are goin' to go into Section I and Section I only. It's a windin' road, an' I figure it will take you about 30 to 45 minutes to circle around and get plenty of pictures. Number two: No drinkin' at all ... zero ... none ... *NADA!* Number three: Last and foremost and above all, don't get out of the car. Do you understand me? DO NOT GET OUT OF THE CAR! These are wild animals, not pets, and they will hurt you."

Scotty, who had a bout with polio in his earlier years, just grinned and replied, "Now, Joe Ed, you know I can't get around very good anyway, so I have no intentions of trying to outrun a wildebeest or a zebra."

"Scotty, it's not you I'm worried about, but Crazy Sam here is a bad influence."

Sam just sat there and chuckled. "Now Doc, you know me; I always do what I'm supposed to and never do anything out of the ordinary."

"Well, this time, you better listen or it could mean your life and my job," I countered, with a relatively serious glare.

"We'll be fine," he assured me. "Besides, what animal in here could be crazy enough to tackle Tarzan and Jane?"

"You're probably right about that, Sam; the pith helmet alone should be a natural deterrent." I got out of the van and then watched them drive through the front gate and off into the sunset. I had a very uncomfortable feeling about the whole thing but, again, I asked myself, *Which animal in Section I would be aggressive enough to actually attack a car or even come to a car?*

The only animal that fit that description was a blackbuck antelope named Dudley. He had been bottle-fed in our nursery, was familiar with humans, and would occasionally charge a car door or put his front feet up under a car window in an attempt to get petted or get food. Dudley had butted a few car doors when he was unsuccessful at getting free food, yet he had been quiet lately. He only weighed about 120 pounds, but he had long spiral horns measuring about 18 inches in length and was learning to use them. Being a typical bottle-fed orphan, with a lack of fear toward humans and with hormones kicking in, his behavior was understandable. Most tourists found Dudley amusing and enjoyed the close contact he provided.

I planned to leave the ranger with an extra radio so that he could stay in contact with "Tarzan" and "Jane" on the radio I had left with them. I tried the radio one time to see if it worked. "How is the safari goin', Tarzan?" I kidded.

"Couldn't be better," Sam answered back. "Everybody is behaving so far."

"I'm outta here. If you need anything, call for John here at the front gate." With that, I handed the radio to the ranger, got into my truck, and then drove off. I figured I had done all I could do, but something kept telling me this wasn't going to turn out OK.

I had been at my meeting in Grand Prairie for about an hour when I got a call from John on my cell phone. "Doc! Doc! Get out here quick or call an ambulance or somethin'. The ladies in the van just called me in hysterics, and the best I can tell is that somebody is badly hurt. They were yellin' and screamin' so loudly I couldn't tell what was goin' on, but I'm headin' out there to find out."

"Call me when you get to their van, and we'll decide what to do. I'm on my way."

About five minutes went by before John called me back. He was at the van and reported that all he could see was Dudley running around the

133

van with a Nikon camera strap wrapped around his horns. The windows were rolled up, and everybody inside looked safe.

"Ask them if everybody is all right."

"They said everybody is fine except Sam, who has been gored by Dudley."

"Do they need an ambulance?"

"No, they don't think so," answered John.

"I'll be there in five minutes."

As I drove up, I could see Dudley still running around the van with the camera attached to his horns. "John!" I shouted. "Grab that crazy blackbuck an' I'll take the camera off the horns!"

Dudley did his usual jumping, pogo-stick antics that blackbucks do when grabbed, but I was able to untangle the camera and get it back to Scotty, who was crouched down in his seat with a sheepish grin on his face. Sam was just sitting there — pale as a ghost — staring straight ahead, too embarrassed to even look at me.

The girls, still shaking with excitement and fear, both yelled at me, "We told them, 'DON'T GET OUT OF THE CAR!' We told them over and over again that you said, 'DON'T GET OUT OF THE CAR,' but you know Crazy Sam — he did it anyway."

"Calm down, girls." I looked at Sam and asked, "Are you all right?"

"I'm OK, I think, but my butt sure is sore."

"What on earth happened?"

"We told them not to get out of the car," both girls chimed in again from the back seat.

"That's true," Scotty confessed. "They told us not to get out of the car, but we had a little problem."

"What problem?"

"First of all," Jane scolded, "we hadn't gone 200 yards before Tarzan decided to get out of the car to get a closer picture of a giraffe with the sunset in the background."

"That seemed to work OK," Scotty added, "so we all kinda lost our fear of getting out of the car."

"No, we didn't *all* lose our fear," Vivian corrected. "We told you guys not to get out of the car!"

"I was the next one to get out," Scotty continued. "A little antelope-looking guy came right up to us and looked gentle enough, so I figured I could get some neat close-ups. He acted harmless."

"Yeah, harmless enough till he took Scotty's camera away from him," Vivian interrupted.

Scotty continued his story. "I couldn't believe my eyes. This little creature was standing there with my Nikon wrapped around his horns like a Christmas tree ornament."

"That would be Dudley, the blackbuck antelope," I interjected sarcastically.

"Well, just who does he think he is, stealing my camera?"

"Joe, we really did tell them not to get out of the car," Becky said apologetically.

"I appreciate that, Becky, but I know these guys, too."

I looked at Sam; he still was just sitting there quietly, staring ahead. It was very unusual for Sam to be so quiet so I began to wonder what else had happened. "Go on guys," I said, and since Sam wasn't talking, that only left Scotty to continue.

"After that little Dudley charged me and scooped up my camera on his horns, I got mad and decided that no half-grown excuse for an antelope was goin' to take my $400 camera. So I just grabbed him by both horns — like your ranger guy did — and tried to get my camera back, but with my hip and all I was no match for him. He slammed me down on the ground and began butting me in the chest. I just couldn't keep him off me."

Sam finally spoke: "When that happened, I had no choice but to go help Scotty. I figured I might be more of a match for Dudley since I had two good legs."

"So, it was basically Tarzan to the rescue," I joked. A movie-like picture popped into my head of Sam baling out of the truck on the driver's side and running around the van in his Tarzan outfit — pith helmet and all — to help his buddy.

"Well, something had to be done." Sam went on. "When I got there, Dudley had Scotty on his back and still had the camera on his horns. I grabbed the antelope by the horns and tried to get the camera, but he rammed me a couple of times and knocked me down, too. I helped Scotty up and asked him what he wanted to do, while I tried to keep Dudley off of us."

"I told him to give the bozo the camera and for us to get outta here before the creature killed us. Sam said that was fine with him and he helped me back into the van. He shut my door, and I was safe at last, except for the girls in the back yelling that they told us not to get out of the car.

"Then I noticed something peculiar: when Sam ran around in front of the car, his pith helmet popped up in the air and he was not far behind it. When he got back in the van, we asked him what happened. He told us that the little devil had horned him in the rear."

Sam was quiet as ever, but I noticed a grimace on his face. "Sam, are you all right? Did Dudley do a number on your you-know-what?"

Sam was holding his rear-end and thigh as though he was in pain. "You know, I guess he got me worse than what I thought." He lifted himself up enough to reveal a pool of blood that by that time had saturated the seat.

"Sam!" I said, "We've got to get you to a hospital!"

"Uh, I guess so."

I suggested he let one of the girls drive, but Sam reckoned he could drive so off they went to Arlington Memorial Hospital with me following. As we left the park, I could only think how my gut feeling had been right all along. I should have followed my instinct instead of trying to be nice to my friends, which put them in danger. I felt guilty and hoped Sam would be OK.

You can imagine the stares from the hospital staff and other patients as "Tarzan" limped into the emergency room with "Jane" helping him. By then, Sam was in a lot of pain and the gored area was still bleeding. Our explanation of how "Tarzan" had been gored by Dudley, a mixed-up blackbuck antelope, left a lot of room for skepticism from the nurses.

After the nurses examined the wound, they sprang into action. The attending doctor deadened the affected area with lidocaine and gently probed the wound. They injected some radio-opaque material into the area and took an x-ray. We were all in shock when, to our disbelief, the puncture wound extended from Sam's lower gluteal area (near the muscles of the buttocks) into his thigh and almost completely out the front — a distance of more than nine inches. The horn had missed the femoral artery by only a few centimeters, and Crazy Sam was very lucky to be alive.

We still all laugh about it to this day when we retell the story to our kids and grandkids, but there was a moral to this story and it was (guess what?): **DON'T GET OUT OF THE CAR!**

Section I during normal daytime hours.

CHAPTER 12

MEXICO

The wildlife park closed in the mid-1980s, and this brought an end to a very important chapter in my life. The drive-through theme park concept had been great and had set the stage for other parks to follow. While the animals had thrived, with reproductive successes without parallel, the park suffered two devastating floods in a five-year period and could not continue. Mother Nature dealt the park and me a cruel blow. Only a few animals were lost in the floods; luckily, each time there had been enough warning so that the animals could be moved to safety. They were relocated to breeding farms, zoos, and other wildlife parks. The rangers, the directors, and other personnel also will be part of my life forever.

I really didn't know what I expected in my life when I was unable to drive out to the park as I had done most days for those 12 years. I did know that my practice would change drastically since my work would become limited to more routine animals such as dogs, cats, horses, cows, and donkeys. I didn't know if there even would be enough exotics out there to justify my using the words "Exotic Animals" in my yellow page ads and on my business cards, but I decided to leave the words in all of my advertising and was very pleasantly surprised to receive at least some exotic work over the following years.

During the next 15 years, I would venture to say that exotics composed about 20 percent of my practice, small animals 50 percent, and horses 30 percent. I kept busy and every time I treated an exotic I found that the experience I had gained from my years at the wildlife park was invaluable.

With a newfound freedom and flexibility in my schedule, I didn't know what to do with my spare time since I had more time on my hands than during those prior years. A call from Mickey Hunt quickly changed that.

"Joe, I know you are probably busy, but I want to pass an interesting proposal by you," Mickey began. "The owners of the zoo in Mexico City have purchased a large number of exotic hoof stock from a private ranch near Nuevo Laredo, Mexico. They need someone to capture the animals and help transport them from Nuevo Laredo to the zoo in Mexico City."

"That sounds good to me, Mick. When do I start?" I blurted out while still trying to control my enthusiasm.

"Well, you better be sure you want to do this before you say yes. This is not going to be an easy task."

"How so? What can be hard about darting animals for shipment? We've done it for years at the wildlife park."

"True, but that was here in Texas. This will be in Mexico where things are handled very differently, as you will probably find out. It also could require one to two weeks away from your practice."

In spite of Mickey's warnings, I eagerly signed on for the task. As it turned out, these exotic animals were responsible for introducing me to a wonderful, new culture and to some amazing people who turned out to be not only unforgettable characters but great friends as well.

How hard could this be? I asked myself as I drove down the highway toward Laredo, Texas. I was fortunate to have a young veterinarian working at my clinic who could cover for me while I was gone, and I also had with me Dr. Gene White, an able-bodied assistant.

Gene and I had been friends for years; he dearly loved adventures and was as excited about this trek as I was. I didn't know the exact numbers of animals that we were supposed to capture, but I did know that it included several species of zebra, brindled gnu, giraffe, blackbuck antelope, eland, waterbuck, and Biesa oryx. Since my Spanish wasn't too good, I had failed to get all of the particulars. Gene's Spanish wasn't much better, but we figured we could manage. The representative from the Mexico City Zoo had promised us plenty of manpower, trucks, and crates. They even offered helicopters, if needed, for us to use to shoot darts from or to help locate the animals.

The fact that they were going to supply helicopters should have been my first clue as to what was in store for us.

Dr. Navieux, a veterinarian who worked at the ranch where the animals were located, met us at the border. At last, a chance to learn all the details about what was going to be involved in this job. As Gene and I drove with Dr. Navieux through the back streets of Nuevo Laredo in an old truck with a poorly constructed antelope crate in the back, the story began to unfold.

"Dr. Cannon, more than 10 years ago the Longoria Ranch here in Nuevo Laredo sold more than one hundred head of various species of hoof stock to the Mexico City Zoo. The zoo paid the ranch about $100,000 for them in advance, since they were getting such a good deal on the price. The problem is that they have never been able to take delivery of these animals because they couldn't find anyone who could, or would, capture them. I guess Johnny Schock, the curator of the zoo, heard about you through the Hunts, and now you are here so the animals can soon be delivered to their new home in Mexico City."

"OK, I have one obvious question: Why haven't these animals been captured an' delivered over this 10-year period?" I wanted to know. "What's the holdup?"

"I don't know, *señor*. I don't understand it myself. For some reason, no one could catch them or get close enough to dart them."

"That doesn't make sense. It can't be the area. I was told they are confined in a relatively small area around the main house."

"You are correct, *amigo*. It is a small area, but many capture people have come to try and all have failed."

"Well, OK, just how big is this house pasture, and what is the terrain?"

"My friend, it is only twenty thousand acres and mainly plains, with some gullies and brush."

I nearly choked on the Dr Pepper I was drinking as I spewed it from my mouth in surprise! About that same time, we hit a pothole, and I managed to spill even more of it down the front of my shirt.

"You've got to be jokin'," I said with some distress. "If twenty thousand acres makes up the small area around the house, then how big is the rest of the ranch?"

"About seventy to eighty thousand acres, I think."

Gene and I looked at each other in disbelief. We had agreed to do this job thinking the animals were in a small area, or "trap," where we could get close to them in some type of vehicle or on horseback — but twenty thousand acres? We were in trouble, and it looked like we had made a long trip for nothing. I was afraid to ask my next question, but I just had to do it. "Are all of the animals we need to capture on these twenty thousand acres?"

"Oh, no, not all of them. Some of them are in the 70,000-acre section."

"Well, that is just great," I said disgustedly. "Gene, we might as well pack up and head back right now!"

"Yeah," Gene agreed, "we might as well do some sightseeing for a couple of days and head home."

"Oh no, amigo, you cannot go," he pleaded. "You are our last hope for someone to help us. You must not go! Please stay and try. I will help you; my *caballeros* will help you. They are experienced animal men."

"Dr. Navieux, I know you mean well, but it just won't work. Even if we have helicopters, that's just too large of an area. Besides, the stress of running the animals would result in losing more than we could safely capture."

By that afternoon, the situation appeared to be growing even bleaker. The new crates they had promised us turned out to be old, broken ones in bad need of repair, and Johnny Schock was having difficulty lining up the choppers. Even getting the two-way radios they had promised us was looking doubtful.

"What have I gotten us into?" I asked Gene over dinner that night.

He smiled. "Don't be so hard on yourself, amigo. Look, we both love an adventure, we are already here, and the cowboys are willing to help, so why not stay a couple of weeks and give it a shot?" Besides that, we further agreed that we were experienced with exotics and probably knew a few tricks the cowboys didn't."

The following morning, we started the 40-mile drive to the Longoria Ranch. The first few miles of dirt road were through typical Old Mexico: flat desert-like country with lots of yucca and scrub brush. As we neared the final gate into the twenty thousand acres surrounding the *casa grande*, or ranch house, the terrain changed. The beautiful prairies and meadows had a slight roll to them, with many patches of scattered timber, and several natural lakes that I could see at a distance. Inside the gate, across the prairie approaching the casa grande, I could see a large cloud of dust heading toward us. Thinking it was a dust devil like we have in Texas, I asked Dr. Navieux how frequently dust devils occur there.

"No dust devil, señor. Animals." Not fully understanding what he meant, I stared at the dust cloud. "Just wait, señor, they come."

And come they did! We slowed down as a herd of some 80 brindled gnu (wildebeest) ran across the road in front of our pickup and then angled away from us. A more beautiful picture I had never seen. I felt like I was in Africa. Gene and I looked at each other in disbelief; we had no idea anything this natural could be seen anywhere other than Africa.

"How long have these wildebeest been on the ranch?"

"Probably 25 to 30 years. The Longoria family had several pairs of almost every species imaginable imported over here to the ranch, and they have run free and flourished ever since."

"They all look healthy," I observed. "How do you vaccinate or worm them?"

"We don't. We just let Mother Nature take its course. We put out salt and mineral blocks, and that's about all we do."

Gene and I shook our heads in amazement. We both understood that, since they were running in such a large area, parasites and disease were probably not a problem.

As we drove on, a group of six or so Chapman zebra ran across our path, as did about 20 Hartman zebra. Even though they were all zebras, the two species were running in their own separate herds, just like in Africa. We had been given orders to capture some zebra, so I thought it might be possible to get a shot at some of them later.

The road made a jog to the left and straightened out along a fence line. On the other side of the fence I could see a large cluster of buildings, some windmills, and what appeared to be a village. Women and children were hanging out laundry and working in their gardens. A few children were playing in the streets, but I saw no men.

"What is that village and where are the men?" I asked Dr. Navieux.

"That village was built for our caballeros and their families so they don't have to leave and go to town. Mr. Longoria even provides schools and teachers for the children. We have second and third generation caballeros living here. We provide all of their meat and staples, and pay them as well. They feel it is an honor to work here and take care of his animals. In addition to the wild animals, we also run many, many cows. Every morning they saddle their horses and ride over into the main pasture in a group. They will be gone all day doing their chores on the ranch, all from horseback."

"How many live here on the ranch?"

"We keep at least 25 here at all times. You will meet them tomorrow when we start on our animal capture."

Gene and I were excited. We both liked horses and horse people since we had horses ourselves and enjoyed riding. We couldn't wait to meet these real live Mexican cowboys.

The three-story casa grande was as elegant as the ranch was big. The house was built out of native stone and was more than 70 years old. It had ivy growing on the walls and looked like a castle or fortress. Gene and I enjoyed the great food and hospitality, and even played some pool and sang songs with the servants. It was a wonderful time; however, I had a restless night, being in a new country, around new people – plus my anxiety about all the unknown factors.

At dawn, Dr. Navieux awakened us, fed us a large breakfast, and then drove us to the front pasture across from the caballeros' village. Everyone was meeting there to get organized for the capture. Johnny Schock was there from the Mexico City Zoo, along with a representative of the Longoria family. Johnny didn't have much to say, nor did he offer an apology to us for failing to deliver the good crates, helicopters, two-way radios, and the abundance of manpower he had promised.

Gene and I had decided we would make the best of the situation. We would try to get the job done with Dr. Navieux, along with four of his assistants, 10 to 15 broken-down crates, and the caballeros, who hadn't shown up yet. We weren't worried about any of the capture equipment or drugs, as we had brought plenty. We just didn't know how we were going to get close enough to dart the animals without the choppers.

Within minutes of our arrival we were back in Dr. Navieux's vehicle being driven over the dirt road in the early morning sunlight. As we bounced along, I couldn't wait for the first sight of wild animals roaming in their natural habitat. It was not animals, however, that caused me to gasp in awe. To our left, in the early morning sunrise, rode 25 Mexican caballeros. They were heading toward the main animal pasture, just as they did every day of their lives.

On this particular day, they were coming to meet us and help with the animal capture, probably just as apprehensive about the whole thing as we were. I watched their every move as they came nearer. They all wore *sombreros*, with each man wearing a little different shape or style. The horses were mostly dark in color (bays and browns), with three or four grays mixed in. All the horses had long manes and tails, and were prancing with heads held high as their frosty breath flowed from their flared nostrils. Each horse and rider was so elegant that I didn't know which one to study the most. As they rode still closer to us, I could see more detail. They all wore chaps and leather vests, and their saddles had long stirrups with toe guards covering their boots.

It was a sight to behold! It was as if two completely different cultures were merging together with a common goal in mind. I couldn't even think about the animals to be captured. All I could do was look at the horsemen and stare.

"Have you ever seen anything like this before in your life?" Gene asked.

"No one would ever believe us if we told them. Look at those ropes. They're no larger in diameter than my little finger."

"Yeah, and there seems to be a lot more rope coiled up. I think their ropes are not only smaller in diameter, but longer, too."

I agreed, and we tried to turn our thoughts back to the task at hand.

"Dr. Navieux, how is this goin' to work?" I asked.

"Dr. Cannon, you are the expert from Texas, and we are looking to you for guidance. My men are expert trackers and ropers. You tell us what to do, and we'll do it. I had what crates we were able to obtain delivered to a point a few miles from here. As we get our hands on the animals, we will have our truckers deliver the crates to us."

I looked at Gene for advice, but he just looked at me and didn't respond. I decided we would start with "Let's do somethin', even if it's wrong!" Gene smiled in agreement; he knew I was quoting my dad.

We had seen more zebra than anything else, so I decided we would begin with them. Gene and I loaded our first dart guns with 4 cc of M-99 and began our search. We had been instructed to capture only the Chapman species (the more common one with the shadow stripe), but I had seen some Grevy mixed in. The Grevy (or mountain zebra) were a larger zebra with narrow stripes; their ears and head were huge, like on a mule. It should be easy to tell them apart.

Gene and I decided to hide in some tall grass in the middle of the prairie and send the vehicles and horses back around the main roads in an attempt to push the herd closer to us. We loaded up a couple of extra darts in case of a miss and took our place in the grass; we were wearing camouflage clothes to be even more inconspicuous. Our adrenalin was flowing as we lay on our backs and looked at the vast Mexico sky.

"I believe this is more exciting than hunting white tail deer," Gene quipped.

"All I know is, I'm not nearly as nervous hunting deer as I am now."

It wasn't long before our tension became even greater. We could hear the thunder of the hooves as the zebra stampeded across the prairie. When they got nearer, we could even feel the ground begin to shake, and it felt like we were in the middle of a stampede. I wondered if the buffalo hunters of the Old West felt like this.

Gene and I looked at each other and then peered up through the tops of the tall grass. What did we see? About 100 yards away an entire herd of zebra was heading straight for us.

"Maybe they'll veer off," I blurted out to Gene.

"Yeah, and maybe they won't!"

Since my capture rifle was for long distance targets and his was for close range, we decided we would stand up when they were closer. Gene would take a close, running shot, and I would take a longer shot after they passed. We hoped this plan would keep us from being trampled. When they were about 25 yards out — heading straight for us — we both stood straight up, guns in hand, and faced our quarry.

I yelled at Gene, reminding him to "Get a Chapman!" The zebra swerved within 15 to 20 feet of us. Gene turned, with a young Chapman in his sights, and shot. The silver dart sunk solidly into the chest of the young mare.

I chose a larger stud running away from me. Scope to my eye, with the powder gun's cross hairs squarely on the butt of the sprinting zebra, I held my breath and squeezed the trigger. I heard the thump and saw the stud jump slightly into the air as the dart disappeared from his hip. Although I knew I had hit him, I couldn't see the dart hanging from the hip.

"Now what are we goin' to do?" asked Gene. "We've got two zebras hit and still runnin' like the devil, headed for some of the thickest brush I've ever seen."

Gene was right. If they made it into the brush, they would be mountain lion food for sure. I managed to get Dr. Navieux on the walkie-talkie and told him that we had hit two and needed help. "Try an' circle the two that were hit and keep them out of the brush and on the prairie if possible," I told him.

I saw in the distance that the darted zebras were already slowing down; the horsemen had circled the zebra I hit. Gene's zebra disappeared in the brush so we focused our minds on catching my zebra. He was still quite mobile, and I realized I had what was called a "bounce out." When my dart hit the apple-butted zebra, it injected a small amount of the drug on impact but then "bounced out" and deposited the remainder of the tranquilizer in the air and on the ground. The insufficient dose only managed to slow him down about 20 percent, so most likely he would be impossible to catch.

Dr. Navieux, quickly summing up the situation, dispatched two of his best riders to me. "Tell them you'll give them five dollars if they'll catch that zebra, and I guarantee you they'll catch him," he promised.

With nothing to lose at this point, I pulled a five-dollar bill from my wallet and yelled at the approaching riders, "Five dollars to whoever catches the zebra!" I waved the bill over my head and yelled in Spanish one of the few words I knew, "Andale, andale!"

They must have understood because both riders flew by me, yelling at their horses and urging them with their spurs. The lead rider reached down and unleashed his lasso. He rotated the long rope, amazingly small in diameter, over his head in a huge, five or six feet loop.

"What will they ever catch with that size loop?" I asked Gene.

"Probably nothing. I know I sure couldn't throw a loop that size, much less catch anything."

The lead rider made a long throw when he got within 15 yards of the zebra. The loop fell only a few feet short, which amazed me. The second rider, as if gauging the other caballero's mistake, rode past him and managed to get a few feet closer than his compadre. It seemed to take forever for the loop to reach the zebra, but the rope settled down perfectly over its head. The caballero quickly dallied his rope to the saddle horn. It was amazing to me that, when the zebra hit the end of the rope, I could actually see daylight beneath the saddle and rider. Gene and I looked at each other in astonishment. I have no idea why the rope didn't break, but it held and the first zebra was ours.

Dr. Navieux already had called the trucks and within minutes a truck with two crates appeared.

The happy rider rode up to collect his bounty, which I gladly paid. "Me got him, me got him!" he beamed. He probably had done what no American cowboy could have; he was proud indeed and rightly so. We finished loading our first zebra and began thinking about how to get the second.

The caballeros had saved us on the first one, but I hadn't figured out how they could help on the second. "Come over here where the trucks are," boomed Dr. Navieux on the radio. I could see the trucks sitting at the edge of the brush a good distance away, so we jumped into the truck carrying the first zebra and headed toward them.

The caballeros all were circled around Dr. Navieux, awaiting instructions and eager to help. "She went into the brush here," he said, pointing to some broken branches.

I can assure you, I could have never found that spot. There were a couple of game trails that led into the brush, and she most likely followed one of them. I knew that I would have to go in because, if we got lucky enough to find her, I would have to give her a small amount of the reversal drug so we would be able to walk her back out of the brush. I communicated this to Dr. Navieux. He agreed and rattled off some Spanish to one of his riders. Lo and behold, the caballero walked right up to me with a big smile and handed me the reins to his magnificent steed. With his eyes fixed on me, Dr. Navieux said, "Choose someone to ride with you, and the two of you will have to bring the zebra out. It's too thick for any more than two to go into the brush."

I felt more than a little apprehensive about this, but I chose the man who missed the first zebra, and he was delighted to go. With a big grin on his face, he headed down the game trail with me close behind. He kept his head down as he was tracking and seemed to know what he was doing. At times the brush was too thick, and we had to lead our horses. We had gone about 400 yards or so, winding left and right, and the hunt was beginning to look futile. We hit an area where the game trail split, and the path we chose ran parallel to the original one. We kept riding and searching.

We wanted to communicate with each other but were hampered by our language barrier. Ironically, it was he who reached out over that barrier, over the vast differences in our cultures, and looked me straight in the eye. With his hand he pointed at me, then at himself, and said, "Me, you ... *companeros*." He smiled and his face beamed with pride.

His sincerity almost brought tears to my eyes. The man did not know me, nor did I him, but he felt in his heart that we were companions, and he was able to get that point across to me. In return, I pointed to him, then to my heart, and said, "Yes. You, me ... companeros." He appeared content as we continued our search.

By this time we were about a half-mile deep in the brush, and I was ready to call off the search and go back. As we rounded the next corner, just as I was about to tell my companero we needed to head back, I caught a glimpse of something in the thick brush. I said, "Amigo, over there." I pointed to a clearing to our right; sure enough, there she was. As we got closer to her, we realized she was still alive. Gene's dart had stuck between the ribs and delivered a full dose of M-99. She was sleeping like a baby.

As I started drawing up a partial dose of M-50-50, my companero put his rope on her neck and dallied the other end to his saddle horn. In only two or three minutes after the drug entered her vein, the zebra stood up and began her pacing-like steps.

"Amigo, andale!" I called out, pointing back toward our starting place.

He knew what to do. The zebra followed him like a foal follows a mare. We headed back down the trail much faster than we came in, and within a matter of minutes she was fully reversed and loaded in the crate. We had successfully captured two zebras on our first day and were proud of it.

Over the next several days, our team managed to capture brindled gnu, blackbuck antelope, giraffe, and nilgai. Our combination of tranquilizers and the caballeros' ropes was working well, but we were getting low on crates and our time was running out. We needed six more

Chapman zebra to complete our order. By this time the zebra herd was fidgety from being spooked by our capture darts, so we couldn't get near them. Since we knew they were still wandering around the 20,000-acres, we had to devise another plan.

Dr. Navieux came up with the idea of herding them into a box canyon and a pen that would be built near the end of the canyon. It seemed impossible to me, but Dr. Navieux felt certain that his men could do it. It would take the better part of a day to drive them around the perimeter and into the trap, so we began the task at daybreak the day before we were to leave.

Dressed in full camouflage and armed with our capture guns and darts, Gene and I took up a post in the brush at the mouth of the canyon so we would be able to release any unneeded animals that might inadvertently fall into our trap. We could accomplish this by merely closing a wire gate, which could be stretched across the canyon. We only had a narrow window of time between the instant we saw that the animals were in the small canyon and our stretching of the gate behind them. We rehearsed our gate-closing technique for a while and then took our positions to wait for the zebra.

Gene and I both were avid whitetail deer hunters, and some of the whitetail bucks that came within only a few feet of us were absolutely mind-boggling. Neither of us had ever been that close to bucks of that caliber. In some instances, the bucks came within 10 to 12 feet before they would shy away from us at the last minute. Most of them would score in the 160 to 180 Boone and Crockett, a system for scoring trophy animals.

"Gene, what are you doin'?" I whispered as I saw him pointing his dart gun at the hip of a large buck.

"Just dreaming. I'll probably never be any closer to something like this again."

A couple of times I thought he was going to dart one anyway, as he kept aiming at some of the larger bucks. "Easy, Gene, our game has stripes today," I jokingly reminded him.

Most of the day passed, and we had seen whitetail deer, nilgai, brindled gnu, blackbuck antelope, waterbuck, and other creatures, but no zebra. I sensed that the numbers of animals were increasing because they were attempting to stay ahead of the caballeros. Sure enough, I began to hear the yells of the approaching riders in the distance. They were fanned out over a wide area; I was unsure how they were going to drive the zebra into this particular canyon.

The day was sunny and warm, the sky was clear, and the anticipation of darting zebra was overwhelming. I never would have dreamed that my veterinary career would bring me to this exciting place. Here we were, sitting at the mouth of a box canyon on a 70,000-acre ranch in Old Mexico, waiting for a herd of zebra to come charging into our trap. I was so excited I almost forgot to get my darts ready.

"Remember, Gene, we only need the Chapman zebra, the shadow-striped ones."

"It's not me you need to worry about! Do those caballeros and Dr. Navieux understand which ones we want?"

"I hadn't thought of that, but maybe it will be OK."

"Joe, between the two of us, we don't know enough Spanish to order supper, so we may be in trouble on this deal."

Gene was right. Behind the stampeding zebra were 25 caballeros who didn't have a clue what to do when they got to where we were. And only God knew which species would show up from the drive. I couldn't believe I hadn't told Dr. Navieux to stay close to me and be our interpreter. It was too late now; I already could see movement of faint stripes coming through the brush.

"Gene, get ready, here they come!" I shouted, as I quickly repeated our plan. "Don't pull the gate shut until all of the zebra are in the canyon and we can see the riders trailing the herd." As they got closer I thought, *This must've been how the cowboys rounded up the wild mustangs many years ago.*

The zebra suddenly exploded from the brush, thundering into the canyon. I tried to make out the species funneling into our trap but, with the dust rising and rocks flying, I wasn't able to recognize even one of the three species. It didn't take long for our canyon pen to fill up since the caballeros had somehow managed to round up every zebra on the ranch!

I yelled to Gene once the fence was in place, "Try to pop three males, and I'll try to pop three females."

"I can't even tell which ones are Chapman, much less what sex they are," he yelled back.

The zebra already were getting extremely nervous because they realized they were trapped. They were biting and kicking each other, racing around the perimeter of the pen, and jumping and running into the fence in an attempt to escape. The dust had settled a little, but we still couldn't make out which ones were Chapman or what sex they were.

"I'm goin' to let some out, an' maybe then we can see the others better," I hollered at Gene. It was dangerous, but I threw open the gate and managed to let out six or seven head who headed straight up the side of a rocky cliff and into the heavy brush beyond. The next thing I knew, three riders took off after the zebra in a dead sprint. They were whipping their horses and riding full speed in hot pursuit of the supposed escapees. I yelled at the riders, "No needie, no needie," but they were already out of sight.

"Never mind, Joe, they'll never catch those wild zebra," Gene said. "Let's just dart these."

After we reduced the number of animals, we could see much better. We got darts in three head each and thought we might even have the right sex. Time would tell on that.

I still was more worried about the riders chasing the zebra. The loyal riders, wanting to please, had assumed that the zebra had escaped and that we needed them back in the pen. Dr. Navieux hadn't arrived yet. The language barrier had become a factor again, but I couldn't worry about it now. We had too much else to do.

The six zebra we darted were starting to stagger, so I decided that, whether they were the right or wrong sex, I would release the remainder of the herd. I was afraid they were going to break their necks the way they were bouncing off the fence, so I felt I had no choice. As I threw open the gate and allowed the extra zebra to dash up the mountain, I could tell that some of the riders understood what was happening, but some of the caballeros still chased zebra up the mountainside and then rode back looking confused.

If only Dr. Navieux was here. I tried to get it across to the riders that we didn't need their help any longer; some understood and some didn't. They talked to each other, and most of them finally got off their horses and helped us with our six darted zebra. The truck arrived with crates, and we were able to get them all loaded. As luck would have it, of our six Chapman zebra, three were males and three were females.

As we finished loading the last zebra, which took about two hours, I noticed a rider approaching out of the corner of my eye. It was my companero, the roping expert, who had chased after the zebra we didn't need. He was prancing up on his horse with a big smile on his face and glowing with pride.

"Me got him, amigo!" As he looked at me with pride, he repeated, "Me got him, amigo!"

"What does he mean, Gene? He couldn't possibly mean that zebra because there's no way he could've caught a wild zebra with no tranquilizer in him. I don't think anybody in this world could've done that."

"Well, he's dang sure got somethin'. He's too proud and happy to be joking."

"Come, amigo," he motioned as he offered to help me up on his horse.

"You better go, Joe. This looks serious," Gene laughed. As I swung up behind my friend and we rode off, he said again with his fist over his heart, "Me, you … companeros."

"Si, si. You, me … companeros," I assured him. We must have ridden two miles into the mountains where the zebra had disappeared, when I began to hear other riders talking in Spanish. I knew we were getting close to the answer to this mystery, but when we came into a clearing, I was not prepared for what I saw. There, in the warm Mexico sun, were the other riders on horseback with a zebra pulled taught between their horses. The men were also glowing with pride over their catch.

It probably never has happened before or since, but they caught up with a zebra and "headed and heeled" him. They had a blindfold over his eyes and had loosened the rope around his neck so he wouldn't choke. They had captured a zebra with no tranquilizer, using nothing more than their ropes, and they were waiting patiently for my orders. It was a big Grevy male and it was beautiful, yet not the species we needed.

I began trying to explain that we didn't need or want this zebra, but they didn't understand. I tried to act out what I needed to say by borrowing a rope from my companero and placing it around my neck, then taking it off, saying, "No needie, no needie."

The riders were terrified at my performance, and I realized they probably thought I was going to hang them for their efforts, which was certainly not the reward they had in mind. I finally resorted to giving each one of them five dollars and saying repeatedly, "*Muchas gracias.*" I walked over and removed the rope from the zebra's head. Then I removed the blindfold and the rope from the feet, allowing the zebra to jump up and dart away in a blur, kicking rocks and dust all over us.

Our safari in Mexico was coming to an end. As we headed back down the trail, I felt honored to have been a part of this gracious culture and could only thank veterinary medicine and the grace of God for allowing me to be a part of a once-in-a-lifetime experience. If I hadn't been on a mission involving exotic animals, I never would have experienced this very memorable chapter in my life.

CHAPTER 13

MILLIE, MAGGIE, AND BARNEY

Those next 15 years of private practice brought many more memorable experiences that I will cherish forever. Although I became more and more focused on racehorses, exotics just kept showing up in my life. I treated adult cougars, lions, primates, snakes, iguanas, raccoons, opossums, sugar gliders, and prairie dogs, just to mention a few. I must admit that some stand out more prominently in my mind than others, and it is the experiences with those patients that I will share with you in more detail.

Holidays almost always were filled with a series of crises, but none surpassed the lady who called me just as I was about to sit down and carve our turkey for Thanksgiving dinner. She was hysterical, so it was difficult to understand what she was trying to tell me in between her sobs and blubbers. I finally figured out that somehow her pride and joy, Millie the canary, was in shock and near death. She evidently was gasping to breathe and had a thick, light brown liquid covering her entire body and beak.

"What is she covered with?"

"Gravy! Gravy!" she yelled. "My Millie is covered in gravy."

After further questioning, I was able to determine that Millie, while flying free in the dining room, had dive-bombed the dinner table and was covered from beak to tail feathers in none other than giblet gravy. The bird apparently had hit the gravy boat with such force that she sank completely out of sight before being rescued by the frantic lady.

After anxiously racking my brain as to what to tell her to do, I finally said, "Put two drops of Ivory liquid in a bowl of slightly warm water and submerge Millie in that solution. Carefully clean the gravy from her mouth and head. Be careful not to get water in the mouth but, if you do, hold Millie's head down and gently drain it out. Wrap her up in a dry, fluffy towel to keep her warm. When she begins to gasp and come back to life, take a Q-tip and clean any remaining gravy from her mouth." The lady proceeded to do all that I recommended, after first asking me to stay on the line in case Millie did not respond.

Moments later, I heard a distant cheer from a crowd in the background as the bird revived and flew off singing, to the apparent surprise of the lady's dinner guests. Millie's owner returned to the phone, explained what had just happened, and expressed her hearty thanks. I told her it was my pleasure. We said our good-byes and I returned to my larger bird, which had by that time grown cold.

Weekends were almost as frantic and bizarre as holidays. Saturday nights were the worst. I sometimes got calls from practical jokers, and one night I thought a particular call was from one of them. It was a Saturday evening around 6:30 when a man's voice — sounding very concerned — informed me, "Dr. Cannon, we've got a big problem here, and I need your help."

"I'll do whatever I can," I answered cautiously. "What seems to be the problem, sir?"

"Well, my fiancée Sally and I were playing with her pet crow, Maggie, and Sally held up her new engagement ring to show it to the bird."

I thought for sure it was another practical joke, but I decided to carry it out to its fullest. "OK, I get the picture, but where do I fit in?"

"Dr. Cannon, you've got to help us. Maggie grabbed the ring right out of Sally's hand, thinking it was something shiny to play with, and gulped it down. We don't know what to do."

I could hear his fiancée crying in the background and I knew crows were notorious for carrying off shiny objects, so this was starting to be believable.

"Are you kidding me? Her crow swallowed a diamond ring?"

"Yes, I am serious! What can we do?"

I didn't have a ready answer for this one. "Well, I guess I need to meet you at my veterinary clinic and examine Maggie so we can decide on a course of action," I said after briefly considering my options.

"All right, we'll do anything. You've got to get this ring back."

I gave him directions to my clinic, and when I arrived they were already sitting in front of the hospital. Once we all were in an examination room, I found Maggie to be a mature crow who was very friendly and full of personality. She obviously had no idea as to the seriousness of her act as she flitted back and forth from the owner's wrist to mine. I managed to hold her quiet just long enough to palpate her abdomen, but I was unable to feel the ring.

The young couple paced about nervously, asking repeatedly, "What can you do? What can we do?"

"First of all, I need to take an x-ray to confirm the size and location of the ring."

"We know it's in there because we saw her swallow it, and its about the size of a dime," the man offered.

"I understand, but I need to know if it's in the crop, the proventriculus — the stomach — or the intestine. That will determine our options."

"OK, go ahead and take an x-ray," he spoke quickly. "We need to know."

The x-ray, which I still have to this day, left no doubt as to the diagnosis. I held up the x-ray for them to see. "Here it is, as big as life, lodged in Maggie's stomach."

"How do we get it back?" Sally asked with a puzzled look on her face.

It was not an easy question to answer. I had to decide how I was going to explain to them that most likely it was going to come down to sacrificing the crow for the ring. Due to the area of the stomach where the ring was located, it seemed unlikely that surgery would be an option. I also doubted they would want to spend the money it would take to do the surgery. I carefully outlined the options, being careful not to be insensitive since I didn't know where they stood on the most likely method of retrieving the ring.

The man understood the obvious scenario and was leaning toward sacrificing the crow for the ring; however, when this picture finally dawned on the fiancée, we immediately found out where she stood.

"You're not about to kill my Maggie for that darned old ring!" she exclaimed. "I don't care what it costs." Maggie flitted around inside a cage and appeared happy when she heard her owner's decision.

The man, on the other hand, was livid. He tried to reason with his fiancée. "We don't have the money for the surgery, and he's not even sure that it will work, that Maggie will live."

"Well, let me put it this way," she countered. "We're trying the surgery or we're not getting married, and that's all there is to it!"

He stared at her in disbelief. I guess he had underestimated how much she loved Maggie.

At that point, realizing the direction this had taken, I agreed to try the surgery. After I explained the risks and the costs, they consented. I began preparations for the task of operating on a crow to remove a diamond ring from her stomach.

Since I had never done this type of surgery, I was more than a little nervous as I gave Maggie her first injection of Ketermine, followed by an inhalation anesthetic. She responded nicely and slipped into a comfortable plane of surgical anesthesia. Soon she was relaxed, and I was able to feel the ring through the abdominal wall. I plucked a few feathers, did a surgical scrub, and made my incision. I recovered the ring quickly; within a matter of minutes I was sewing up Maggie's stomach lining and suturing her skin. The surgery was completed, and since Maggie had received only a few sniffs of the inhalation anesthetic (due to the high metabolism that all birds have), she already was coming around nicely.

The woman was ecstatic to see Maggie moving around and to hear me say she would probably live. The man was more than happy to have the ring back in his hand. As it turned out, Maggie made a successful and uneventful recovery, and the couple did get married.

The routine around the clinic would stay fairly quiet for a while, but then something out of the ordinary would occur.

One day I received a call from my old friend, Dr. Jack Brundrette. "Dr. Jack" was the veterinarian for the Dallas Zoo; he and I consulted with each other on occasion so it came as no great surprise when he asked me to help him with a patient. Jack also had a private practice and did some work for an individual who had a traveling bear act. Evidently one of the bears had a problem.

Jack could be a bit of a practical joker, so when he told me he had a grizzly bear with an abscessed tooth, I first thought he was joking.

"Joe, I'm out here at Brinkman's and have immobilized this bear to examine him and found out that I need to pull one of his molars."

"Yeah, right, and I've got a giraffe with a sore throat," I answered in jest.

"No, I really do. I'm only about 15 minutes from your clinic."

"OK, how can I help, Jack?" I tried to sound as gullible as possible so I could find out where he was going with this prank.

"The bear is asleep from the Sernalyn (an anesthetic used as an immobilizing agent) I gave him through the dart gun, so he'll start wakin' up in about 30 minutes unless I maintain him on a gas anesthetic machine. Since you have one, I need to borrow it bad."

"Jack, you sound convincing, but this is too far-fetched. How in the world are you goin' to get a full grown grizzly bear to my clinic? And what will my clients do when you bring that bear through the waiting room and into my surgery room?"

"Joe, I'm not pullin' your leg this time. I'm dead serious! Couldn't we work on him in that fenced area out back of your clinic? You could bring the anesthetic machine out to us."

"All right, but if you're messin' with me, I'm goin' to dart you with Sernalyn."

"You'll see, Joe. I'm on my way!"

By that time he had convinced me that perhaps he wasn't joking. I started to plan how I would make this work. I had to prepare for the worst; I moved my anesthetic machine outside and opened the door to my backyard. Next, I alerted all of my technicians.

Within about 10 minutes, I started to hear sirens and couldn't imagine what that could be about. Since the sirens were getting closer, I walked to the front of the clinic and looked out a window. A police car pulled into my parking lot, followed by a white car and another police car, but I didn't see any truck with a bear cage.

What I did see, however, almost put me in shock. There, between the police cars, was Jack's old white Volvo. Jack was driving with an unrecognizable passenger sitting along beside him, and two people in the back seat. *But who in the dickens was the passenger?* He looked like a large, hairy man wearing a felt hat and leaning back in his seat.

The thought occurred to me again that this really was one of Jack's pranks. *What is Jack up to this time? He really has gone all out with the police escort.*

Jack drove around and backed right into the area I had made ready for him, but I certainly was not prepared for what happened next. He started honking his horn like a wild man. I ran outside and hollered, "Jack, have you gone crazy?"

Jack was already out of his Volvo. He opened the door on the passenger side and said, "Joe, meet Mr. Barney Bear." Lo and behold, reclined in the car seat was the anesthetized grizzly bear with a hat pulled down over his eyes. I was speechless!

Jack laughed at me. "Well, don't just stand there, let's get his tooth pulled. I don't have all day and neither do these policemen." In his own sly way, Jack had done it to me again, but this time by telling me the truth, the real story.

"You should've seen the looks I was gettin' comin' over here," he said with a wide grin. "Two or three people nearly ran off the road."

"I can understand that. It's not every day you see a grizzly bear in a Volvo, asleep or otherwise."

Although he was relaxed, Barney was starting to move his front paws slightly. I hurried up with the mask and placed it tightly over his nose. After a few big breaths, he was snoring like a buzz saw.

Because of his weight, we decided to use the reclined Volvo seat as a dental chair. His jaw was very swollen, and I could see and smell the abscessed tooth, which already was almost black. Using my dental instruments, along with some drilling, we were able to get the tooth out with the roots intact. We flushed the socket with an antibiotic solution and gave Barney a large dose of penicillin in the hip. He was good to go.

Jack thanked me as he packed the socket with gauze, put Barney's hat back on, and jumped in the driver's seat. "Got to hurry, Joe. He's goin' to start comin' around pretty soon. See ya."

What an afternoon this has been. I walked back inside the clinic. This was absolutely a once-in-a-lifetime event, just like so many of my other experiences with animals.

CHAPTER 14

DOTTIE

The years passed quickly, and with each year there were enough exotic patients to maintain my enthusiasm and keep my diagnostic and surgery skills sharp. Although I enjoyed treating the exotics more than my other patients, I didn't know if it was because of my relationship with Silky and Red when I was growing up or if it was purely out of respect for their intelligence and beauty.

As I became older and the numbers of exotics that I was treating declined, I began cultivating my equine skills, treating more and more horses.

I guess it was because I had been a farm boy that I just couldn't get the large animals out of my blood. I'm probably a perfect example of the old adage: *You can take the boy out of the country, but you can't take the country out of the boy.* I treated all types of horses, ranging from the backyard pet to thoroughbred and quarter racehorses.

The racehorses held a certain fascination for me. There was something special about watching and being around animals that were trained to do what they were meant to do naturally, and that was to run. Racehorses enjoy running. Sure, some are faster than others, but they all seem to love to run down that track. Most of my daily veterinarian work performed on these animals was comprised of giving injections, doing lameness exams, taking x-rays, and occasionally doing some type of minor surgery.

My days started around five o'clock in the morning and ran well into the evening, especially on the days of the races. The sale of my veterinary clinic in 1999 left me working as a solo, mobile equine practitioner. Since I had no clinic where exotic animals and pets could be brought for treatment, my wild animal practice dwindled away. I just about had given up on treating any more exotics when God blessed me with one more beautiful creature to treat.

People say history repeats itself, and we were told in vet school that the country boy spends the first half of his life getting out of the country and away from all of that hard work. Then, the last half of his life is spent trying to get back to the country life to enjoy the very things he walked away from in the beginning. I was a sterling example of this tenet. I worked so hard on the farm until I couldn't wait to get to the city to make my fortune and enjoy my career. I had to admit, though, that while in the city I was allowed to enjoy my profession by seeing and treating animals that I would have never known existed if I had practiced in a country town.

As I grew older, however, I began to tire of the hustle and bustle of the crowded conditions of the Dallas-Fort Worth Metroplex. I began to long for the quiet summer nights when I slept outside where the only sounds I heard were the crickets and the coyotes howling. I missed the days when I romped and played with Silky and Red, and I just plain longed to be in the country and around country folks. It was as if I had accomplished all I could in the city; it was time to slow down and enjoy nature and life in general.

Sharyn, my wife of 23 years, and I talked it over and decided to buy some land so we could gradually move to a quieter lifestyle. We purchased 350 acres in the sleepy little community of Desdemona, Texas — population 30. The irony of this was that it was only 20 miles, as the crow flies, from the community of Greens Creek where I grew up.

The ranch was perfect for us. It was definitely in the country, was quiet, and literally abounded with wildlife. Even if I couldn't treat these creatures as patients, I could at least be around them. Whitetail deer, wild hogs, wild turkey, quail, and dove made this ranch their home. There also were foxes, coyotes, owls, hawks, and numerous songbirds to be found. When I was here with all these animals around me, I felt at home.

I ran advertisements in the yellow pages of telephone books published in the surrounding towns and slowly began treating all types of animals in this area. Horses were my mainstay, but I also treated donkeys, goats, cattle, cats, dogs, and just about any other animals that came along.

The largest horse farm I serviced was a cutting horse ranch located in Lipan, Texas, called the Diamond B Ranch. At one time, they ran more than a hundred head of cutting horses and usually kept me pretty busy. The young couple in charge of the day-to-day operation of the ranch, Duff and Billie Jo Sinclair, over the months became good friends of Sharyn and mine. They both were very hard working people and seemed to really have a way with the horses, genuinely caring about them.

Billie Jo was originally from Oregon but was adapting well to becoming a Texan. She possessed a special knack for nurturing baby animals and was always full of questions about whatever young calf, dog, cat, or bird she might have come across during her daily routine. She was very strong willed, and whatever she set her mind to doing usually got done, so most of her nursery projects were a success.

It was about mid-May at the Diamond B, and we were in the middle of the breeding season, trying to finish getting almost 40 mares bred and in foal. In most cases horses don't need any help breeding, but with modern technology and the advent of shipped semen, artificial insemination was commonplace. The mares' ovaries had to be checked via ultrasound on a daily basis so we would know the exact time that the frozen, or cooled, semen should be implanted into the uterus. Not only could you breed more horses at one time, you also could breed a mare to a stallion thousands of miles away.

This high-tech breeding was responsible for our routine during the months of February through June. By May, however, everyone was starting to get out of sorts with each other, which was typical for this stressful time of year. The last thing we needed was any distractions from the job at hand, which was breeding mares. Duff recently had hired a new hand to help during this busy time, and the new hand still was trying to learn all of the ins and outs of his new job. He got distracted easily and acted impulsively on occasion, but we all were trying to deal with that. His name was Kevin and, as it turned out, he was directly responsible for the events that unfolded over the next few months.

The Diamond B was a beautiful ranch of about 1,600 acres near Lipan, a small town located in the north central area of Texas. The ranch itself was mostly open grassland with a few live oak thickets and around a hundred or so acres of post-oak timber. Like my ranch, the Diamond B abounded with wildlife that included turkey, quail, dove, wild hogs, and whitetail deer. We had received a lot of rain for May; the grass and pastureland was lush, tall, and green. There were about 70 head of cattle on this place, but that didn't make a dent in the abundance of grass.

I often would spot deer while driving across the ranch through a couple of areas where they appeared to be residents. There was one area where you might see at least two very large does bedded up by the road. For some reason they liked this spot and felt secure there, even though a road ran right by their bedding ground. I frequently stopped to watch them for as long as they would allow me the privilege. To see them with their slick, brown bodies and big, brown eyes standing in a field of wildflowers and lush grass was a beautiful sight to behold.

Deer usually breed from August to January; since their gestation period was about seven months, I knew these does were either getting ready to have babies or already had some hidden nearby. Deer, like cows, meticulously hide their newborn for a week or so until they are strong enough to tag along with mom. The does will bed down their offspring in a very secure spot and then may leave for several hours before returning to allow them to nurse. The white spots on the fawns blend in perfectly with the small white wild flowers, and their coats make perfect camouflage to keep predators from finding them. Yet, in spite of the care and precautions, a large number of fawns are killed every year by coyotes. If a young deer can make it to three to four weeks of age, it has a very good chance for survival.

Although I was curious whether the does had fawns, I didn't dare go near them for fear of spooking a doe away or spooking the fawn if it was lying nearby in the grass. When young calves or young deer are spooked, they will jump up hysterically, run blindly, and become fearful that predators are attacking them. It is another of nature's mysteries how a doe can hide her fawn in a certain spot, wander off for miles, come back in several hours to the location where she left her baby, and find it laying in the exact spot and position it was in when she left. Some young people don't know this, and their carelessness has resulted in many orphan fawns.

It was a busy morning at the Diamond B; we had about 20 mares to palpate and examine with ultrasound to determine where they were in their cycle. Duff would lead each mare into a stock (similar to the squeeze chute used for cattle), and Billie would wrap their tails and wash them in preparation for palpation. When we determined the size and location of the follicles, she would write this critical information into her breeding book so we would have a permanent record to refer to when projecting the ovulation time.

On this particular morning, we were already running behind schedule so Kevin, our new hand, had been sent to the other side of the ranch to pick up some breeding hobbles. They were used to restrain the mare while we were using her to collect semen from the stallion artificially. These hobbles kept her from kicking and injuring the stud during the collection process. Kevin had been gone for more than an hour, and we couldn't figure out what had happened to him.

About that time, the barn door flew open and in burst Kevin. "You're not going to believe this story," he said with a big smile on his face.

"Where in the world have you been?" Billie Jo scolded. "We needed those breeding hobbles an hour ago."

I was pretty upset with Kevin myself since we had been forced to stop the entire operation and sit and wait for him. "This better be a good story," I added curtly, "because you have really held us up this morning."

"Doc, you'll be proud of me. I have been out doin' my good deed for the day." He then retreated back to his truck and quickly returned to the breeding shed with a burlap bag. I noticed the bag had something moving inside of it, and the first thing I thought of was a snake.

"You better not have a rattlesnake in that bag." I snapped. Kevin was young, in his mid-20s, and mischievous, so nothing he ever did surprised us.

"It's not a snake, Doc."

With that he opened the sack, and to my utter dismay and regret, out hopped a whitetail fawn. It was probably only about three or four days old and still a little wobbly on its legs.

I got pretty angry inside for several reasons. First of all, Kevin had held us up for over an hour. Second, he had committed the unpardonable act of making an orphan out of a healthy fawn that would have been just fine without his interference. Third, I knew Billie Jo would fall in love with it and want to raise it, which unfortunately would pose a problem.

The game laws of Texas prohibit the raising or keeping in captivity of any wild game animal such as a whitetail deer. These laws are strict. This deer could not be kept in captivity without a permit from the state, and the state issues very few permits. I realized that Kevin didn't know any of this, but he had created a large problem. There stood a pretty, sleek, spotted little fawn with big eyelashes and soft brown eyes. Billie Jo already had closed her breeding record book and was walking toward the fawn.

Still, hoping there might be chance to reverse what was going on, I hollered at Kevin, "You've got to take this fawn back to where you found it right now."

He looked at me in astonishment and said, "I can't because the mother abandoned it. I saw her running around in the field by herself."

"Which field?" I asked.

"In the low area before you get to the tank."

"Kevin, this fawn wasn't abandoned because I saw two does in that area this morning, and I guarantee you one of them is its mother."

"Well, the mother wasn't around, an' I think it's an orphan."

Billie Jo was getting closer with each step to the baby deer. "Oh, Doc, look at her. Look how sweet she is. Look at those eyes. She needs us!" she exclaimed as she knelt down and picked up the little fawn. By now, it was scared and shaking.

I knew we were all in a mess, one that should never have happened.

Duff, who had been quietly watching this ordeal unfold, understood that raising this fawn was going to be a problem, especially since his dad was a game warden. He knew the game laws and, unlike Billie Jo, realized the situation was even more complicated.

"OK, guys, let's stop discussing this and just take it back to the area where it came from," Duff commanded. "I saw two does there this morning myself, and maybe one will come back to it."

Although that sounded like a good solution, I knew it wouldn't work because once human hands have handled a newborn animal the chances of the mother accepting it back are two-fold: slim and none.

"It just won't work," I interjected. "Kevin, if only you hadn't picked it up. Why did you?" I just couldn't stop scolding him even though I knew the damage was done and nothing could be gained by blaming him.

"I just did. It looked so helpless an' lonely."

I finally admitted to myself the fact that what was done was done, and we needed to decide what to do about it. I had seen bottle-raised deer before and knew there was an ugly side of that, too. People have raised them in the country when similar circumstances lead to that, but when they are grown, then what happens? They are game animals so, when every fall hunting season comes around, what do you do with a deer of either sex that is gentle, a pet, and not afraid of people? How do you reintroduce it back into the wild, and how do you keep it from being shot? I had seen pink ribbons and bells tied around their necks; I also had seen them kept in pens, but neither of those were good options for orphan deer. Most people haven't seen all facets of this situation and can't picture what lies ahead for the baby deer. They only see this helpless, beautiful little critter standing there and looking up at them with those big brown eyes.

With all of these thoughts running through my mind, I finally said, "Duff, we can't take it back with the human scent on it because the mother won't accept it even if she comes back. It would be left there as coyote bait for sure. You better talk to your father about getting a permit."

"Doc, I'll keep it and raise it, and it can be my baby," grinned Billie Jo. Regrettably, that was the only solution.

"Duff, we'll have to do the best we can," I conceded, "and maybe we can reintroduce her into the herd when she's about six months old." I knew he had a problem with it just like I did, but he seemed resigned to the task at hand.

"All right, Doc, whatever you say," he said as he trudged out the door. Kevin, finally understanding what he had done, lowered his head and left the shed. That left me, Billie Jo, the fawn, and about 15 mares to palpate.

"Let's put it back in the sack for now and finish these mares."

She put the little deer back into the sack and found a place under a heat lamp. She opened the sack, placing some straw around the bag. We continued our work with the mares.

Later she brought it into the office and asked, "Is it a boy or a girl, Doc?"

"It is a little doe, Billie Jo," I rhymed, which made me smile as I was beginning to get over my frustration. The beauty and innocence of this little creature almost brought tears to my eyes as I was reminded of past years at the wildlife park and the numerous babies we had to bottle feed and nurse back to health. It seemed like yesterday, but it had been almost 35 years ago. I felt old at that moment. I knew it would be a challenge to raise her, but I also knew I had the knowledge to help Billie Jo and increase her chances of success.

Remembering back to the days of Silky, Squeaky, Football, and other orphans we raised at the park, I was able to come up with a formula that had worked well in the past. It was simple, really, and consisted of half Carnation milk and half water. This mixture was very nutritious and, at the same time, not too rich or high in fat. I told Billie Jo to go to Stephenville and buy a baby bottle to use with a lamb's nipple. I knew the female ewe has about the same size teat as a doe, so in my experience this combination had worked well before. Billie Jo came back with all that was needed; we were ready for our first feeding.

"We might as well go ahead and name her since she is probably going to be around for awhile," I suggested.

"Doc, I've already got that covered. I'm going to call her Dottie. It took me a second for that to register; then I figured how she came up with name. With all of those beautiful white spots that Mother Nature gave her for protection, it made perfect sense to call her Dottie.

Our first attempt at feeding her was a disaster. Dottie was, of course, frightened and didn't have a clue who we were or what our intentions were. She jumped around so much that when we tried to hold her still, I was afraid she was going to break a leg. Dottie was kicking and shaking her head — more milk was getting on Billie Jo and Dottie than in her mouth.

However, she seemed to be secure with the little sack that we had made for her bed, so I suggested we wrap her in it like a towel and then try to feed her. By sitting on her knees and holding Dottie between her legs in her lap, Billie Jo managed to get about one ounce of the formula down. I showed her how to keep the fawn's head at the proper angle to prevent inhalation of the milk. At least none of the milk went into her lungs.

I knew Billie Jo would have her taking a full bottle in no time. And sure enough, that's what she did. She initially fed her small amounts (one-half ounces) several times a day, and soon she was able to feed her about two ounces three times a day as Dottie got older.

Over the next three months, Dottie flourished. I have never seen an animal grow as fast as she did, and I have never seen an animal and

Billie Jo and Dottie at feeding time.

a human develop a bond as fast as those two did. Billie Jo converted an empty horse stall into a nursery. She bedded it with good, clean coastal hay and even placed Dottie's old security tow sack in there. Dottie would bed down on it and burrow into the hay until all you could see sticking out was her velvety ears, her two big brown eyes, and her long, black nose. Billie Jo chose not to make the stall a prison, so after Dottie was a couple of months old, she would leave the stall door cracked in order to tempt Dottie to come and go as she pleased. It amazed me how Dottie would wander around all day, following Billie Jo here and there, and then go back to her stall at some point to lie on her sack.

For the most part, Billie Jo and Dottie were inseparable. If Billie Jo was on the four-wheeler feeding the horses, Dottie rode right along with her. If we were palpating mares, Dottie thought she was helping us by watching. As long as she could see or smell Billie Jo, she was content. I think Dottie actually thought Billie Jo was her mother.

As you can see in the next picture of her feeding Dottie, it was not uncommon for Dottie to find an ear lobe to nurse upon until Billie Jo got a bottle up to Dottie's mouth. This was quite a change from that first day of feeding when a wild animal met humans for the first time. How had this bond become so strong between animal and human? What had caused the fear of humans to go away? Was it need, habit, environment, or just plain survival?

Dottie bonding with Billie Jo.

Dottie had known her doe mother for just a short time and only had known her human mother for a couple of months, but if she were forced to choose now between her mother and Billie Jo, I believed she would choose Billie Jo. With this human bond, would she ever be able to be reintroduced into the wild, and if not, what would become of her?

During the following months, Dottie's features began to change. She was almost four months of age and starting to show signs of maturity. Her face and nose were getting thinner. Her ears were noticeably larger. Her spots were becoming lighter; there was actually an optical illusion caused by the brown hair rapidly growing in between the white ones at about the same time as the white hairs were beginning to turn darker. Although still very attached to Billie Jo, Dottie slowly began to wander farther and farther from her protective area and began staying out of her stall until after dark. During the day, Dottie could be found romping and playing with some of the younger foals.

The adaptability of wild animals has never ceased to amaze me. As far as I was concerned, the increasing independence of Dottie was a positive thing. This could mean there was a chance for reintroducing her to her deer family. Our hopes for that brightened even more when along in September Dottie was seen grazing with a small group of deer near Duff and Billie Jo's house. The only problem was that when Dottie would try to go up to the other deer and play, she was greeted with fairly aggressive head-butts from the larger deer. I'm sure the strange actions and foreign smell of Dottie created a sense of fear and survival instinct within the wild deer group. When Dottie became tired of the rejection, she would graze close by the deer for a while and then she would eventually find her way back to her stall and security sack.

One evening when I was out at the ranch to palpate some mares, I asked, "How is Dottie doin'?" I knew that was the wrong question to ask when big tears welled up in Billie Jo's eyes.

"She didn't come home last night."

I had tried to prepare Billie Jo for this development from the beginning, but no amount of preparation can help when reality sets in. I had explained to her that probably one of three things would happen. One, Dottie would simply not show up one day, and Billie Jo would never know what had happened to her. Two, she might reintroduce herself to a deer family and not come back. And three, she could suffer some unfortunate accident caused by man or some predator. Billie Jo had assured me many times that she understood and was prepared for this day, but I could tell she wasn't.

"Billie Jo, at her age, this is not uncommon," I said, trying to comfort her. "As independent as she is getting, I think it's a good sign that she is staying gone longer. Maybe she has gotten back with the deer herd."

"Yeah, I guess so," she mumbled as she choked back the tears.

I sympathized with Billie Joe and I momentarily recalled the day years ago when I finally had to give up Silky and return him to the wild. I definitely could feel her pain. There can be such a strong bond between a human and an animal.

"You know, it's gettin' close to the fall of the year and Dottie may be hearing the call of the wild," I said, trying to further console her.

I finished checking on the mares, but while driving home that evening I couldn't help but wonder what had happened to Dottie. Early the next morning, my curiosity was eliminated by a phone call from Billie Jo.

"Doc, she's back! Dottie is back, but she's hurt an' she's hurt really bad." I could hear the concern in her voice and knew Dottie had a problem. I had found out early on if Billie Jo called with a problem, it was usually a big problem.

"What is it? Tell me what's wrong."

"Her right front leg is just dangling and flopping, and she has some scratches on her leg."

"OK, I'll be there as soon as I can get there," I assured her before I jumped into my truck and headed to Lipan. I knew from the symptoms she described, Dottie's leg was probably broken. How were we going to handle Billie Jo if I had to put her down? The real question, however, was how would I be able to put her down since I was just as attached to her as Billie Jo was?

Duff and Billie Jo met me at the truck as soon as I arrived. Duff looked worried, and Billie Jo was in tears.

"Doc, I know it's broken," she sobbed. "What are we goin' to do?"

"Let's look at it first and then we'll decide."

"OK, but hurry," Billie Jo said as she ran toward the stall.

I looked at Duff, and even though no words were spoken we both knew we had a problem on our hands and there wasn't going to be a good solution. By the time Duff and I got to the stall, Billie Jo was already there on her knees, holding Dottie's head in her hands. Dottie was holding her right front leg several inches off the ground. Every now and then she would nibble on Billie Jo's earlobe like she used to when she was a little fawn. Dottie made a little, startled jump when she saw me, and as she did her leg just flopped.

I got tears in my eyes as I had a flashback from years ago to Ellie, the elk, and knew immediately that our worst fears were confirmed. Dottie's leg was definitely broken. As I gently touched her injured leg, I could feel the fracture. It was broken about three inches below the knee. There was no bone protruding so it was not compound, but it was a nasty break. In looking into Dottie's eyes, I could tell she was in severe pain and probably had been for many hours. She was showing advanced signs of stress and not far off from shock.

"It's sure broken, Billie Jo. It looks like from the claw or bite marks on her skin that coyotes probably chased her into a fence and then tried to kill her."

"All right, Doc, so let's fix it," she came back instantly.

I looked at Duff for answers. He looked back equally frustrated and, like me, at a loss for words. We all three remained standing in silence for what seemed like several minutes, but in reality was only a few seconds.

"Billie Jo, there is just nothin' I can do. Her leg is smashed. In her condition I don't think she could handle any type of splint or cast. I'm not even sure she can survive any longer in this stall, and this probably means she can never be reintroduced into the wild since she will always have a limp. Even if the leg heals, it wouldn't be fair for her to be caged forever and limp around in pain for the rest of her life. It just wouldn't be fair."

"Billie Jo, Doc is right. I think it's time to stop her suffering," Duff added as he gently put his arm around her to try to console her.

I would have thought Billie Jo would have grown very upset by that time, but she had managed to remain calm.

"I'm not goin' to put her down. I'm just not," Billie Jo answered emphatically. "Even if I have to take her to another vet or fix it myself, I'm not goin' to put her down."

Duff and I both knew it was no use to argue with her. She was stubborn and determined; it was these same two traits that were responsible for getting Dottie to this point, and for that you had to admire the woman.

I backed up, took a deep breath, and searched for an answer. It was as though my prayers were answered as my mind again was taken back to Ellie. I suddenly could hear the voices in the treatment room that day pleading for me to give Ellie a chance. I had given Ellie that chance against all odds, and furthermore it had worked.

"Oh, OK, I guess we can go ahead and try," I relented, "but there's no guarantees, and she might not even survive the anesthetic since she's so shaky."

Dottie's ear tips and legs were already cold, which indicated that shock was setting in rapidly. When this happens, a large portion of the blood pools in the intestinal tract; the extremities and brain do not get enough blood, and this usually causes death. I knew the anesthetic would further add to her shocky condition, so I decided to give her an intravenous dose of Soludelta Cortef. After I gave her 3 cc of this anti-shock medication, I gave her .6 cc of Telazol (an anesthetic) intravenously.

Dottie relaxed in Billie Jo's arms, lying there quietly with her big brown eyes staring up at us. I could hardly keep back the tears as I expected Dottie to make her last gasp at any moment, but she didn't.

She even began to breathe deeper and more regularly. For the time being, at least, it all was working.

"See, Doc, she's fine," Billie Jo said optimistically. "I knew she would be."

"So far, so good, I guess. I'm goin' ahead and pick up her leg and try to set it by pulling hard, so hold on to Dottie while I pull."

"Go ahead and pull. I've got her."

As I pulled and tugged, I could feel her crumpled bone and mangled skin stretch and pop as the two ends of the bone came together. I still didn't know how good the blood supply was to the bottom part of the foot; I could only hope and pray that an artery or vein hadn't been severed.

Dottie in her new cast.

"There, it's back together. Hand me that splint, Duff, if you would." I slid the padded, half-shell splint on her leg and all the way up past her "elbow." I couldn't allow any movement in the entire leg or all would be lost. The cast was a perfect fit. Things were moving along well. Since the fracture was not compound, I didn't have to be too worried about infection, but I gave her a large dose of antibiotics anyway and then followed that by giving her the reversal drug to wake her up.

Billie Jo's eyes had begun to look happy by this time. A little smile was creeping across her face as Dottie started to wiggle and shake her head much like a newborn fawn might do when first trying to stand up after birth. After a couple of minutes of head bobbing and shaking, she simply stood right up on her new cast and looked around at us.

This was the moment of truth because most wild animals will not tolerate a cast, will simply freak out and run into things until they kill themselves. I had my fingers crossed when, lo and behold, she took a few steps on the cast and immediately went over and started nursing on Billie Jo's earlobe. This was her way of saying she was hungry. I looked at Duff; we both knew we had made the right decision.

We kept Dottie confined to her stall for the next 45 to 50 days and then came the next true test. It was time to x-ray the leg to see if the fracture had healed. Dottie had continued to eat and drink well. There had been no sign of infection. I felt reasonably sure that the blood supply had returned to the foot. But had the bone itself healed?

"Well, look at this," I said as I beamed, showing the x-ray to Duff and Billie Jo. "It looks like new."

"Let's take that old cast off so she can play," Billie Jo said excitedly.

"We can take it off, but we'll have to keep her confined for one more week to make sure it's going to hold," I said.

Dottie was as eager to get the cast off as we were. She kicked and nibbled at the newly found leg that she hadn't seen for a while. She still

Dottie — free as a deer should be.

held it up a little, favoring it, but that was to be expected since she hadn't really felt it and used it for nearly two months. After about an hour, she began touching her toe to the ground, and within another hour she was putting almost all of her weight on it. Thanks to God, it was truly a miracle!

After her last week in solitary confinement, so to speak, we cracked her stall door and allowed her the same freedom that she had before.

Well into the fall, Dottie had grown, in spite of her cast, into a fairly large doe. Her spots were completely gone, and like before she began staying away longer and longer. I think Billie Jo was prepared for this by that time and — after literally saving her life — she felt she had done all she could toward reintroducing Dottie back into the wild.

That year and in the following years the hunting season came and went, and occasionally Duff or Billie Jo would see a group of deer with one doe lingering behind, staring back toward the barn for a long period of time. They were certain it had to be Dottie. I'm certain they were right.

Even though Dottie was safe and happy with her new deer family, I'm sure she will always remember her foster mother. I'm more than sure that Billie Jo will never forget her.

Oh, by the way, there is NO HUNTING allowed on the Diamond B Ranch!

CONCLUSION

LOOKING BACK

As I reflect back on my 35 years of veterinary practice, it makes me feel good inside to know that, in some small way, I was able to help the animals that I came in contact with to have a better quality of life. I enjoyed caring for each one of them, but I will have to say that the exotics will always hold a special place in my heart. Their beauty, intelligence, cunning, and wild nature make them special, setting them apart from all other animals. I also feel that these animals directly affected the lives of everyone who interacted with them on a daily basis, such as the rangers and wardens who worked at International Animal Exchange. Many of these animal caretakers have gone on to be very successful zookeepers and curators. Ray Sutton, Kurt Giesler, and Ron Surratt are examples of this lifelong devotion to exotics.

Ray Sutton, a senior ranger, came from the park in Ohio to work in Texas for the last five years before it closed. Ray had a marvelous way with animals and I wish I could have had the opportunity to work with him longer. From this photo you

Ray Sutton and his buddy.

can see that Ray loved to carry his lion friend, Bruno, with him whenever he could. I'm not sure who was having more fun, him or the lion. Ray is still working with International Animal Exchange and has given a lot of himself to the animal world.

Kurt Giesler, like Ray, was another transfer from the park in Ohio and also came on board with us in Texas for the last five years prior to the

Kurt right home in Texas.

closing. He had tremendous knowledge of animals and a special way with them, as noted in the photo. When you can break a 4,000-pound white rhino to ride, you have certainly earned your spurs and the right to be called a cowboy. Kurt still lives in Texas and is a curator at the Fort Worth Zoo, but I'll venture to say that this was the first and last white rhino he will ever ride. I didn't even try that, and I'll try just about anything!

Ron Surratt, another senior warden at the park, became the head curator of the Fort Worth Zoo after the wildlife park closed. There he continues the work he loves so much. Ron pulled me out of a lot of scrapes while we were working together, and I will forever be indebted to him. Ron was almost killed by a leopard while making his rounds at the zoo, but to this day he still shares the same respect and admiration for exotics that he always did.

It's hard to say to what degree my children were influenced by being around some of these animals, yet I believe that being able to touch a small zebra or a baby ostrich, as my daughter Amy is seen doing in the photograph, has certainly made a lasting impression on her. Amy still enjoys animals to this day, and I hope she looks back on the summers at

The nursery attendant helping Amy and Chad with bottle-raised Hartman zebra.

Amy with ostrich chick.

the park as a rewarding experience.

Although Chad and Troy interacted with many of my animal friends, I'm certain that the time they spent with Judy was their most memorable. It is not often that a child has the opportunity to go "trick-or-treating" with a movie star chimpanzee.

Today, Chad is an attorney, Troy is a sales representative for a pharmaceutical company, and they both have pets they love very much. I can only hope their childhood experiences with animals were positive ones, and that these early contacts with animals helped make them the animal lovers they are today.

178

My sister, Linda, shared my excitement for the exotics and loved to come from Amarillo to visit and ride with me on my rounds. She enjoyed taking photographs of the animals and of me treating them. In fact, she is responsible for many of the photos in this book. Since she was used to hard farm work when she was growing up and didn't mind getting her hands dirty, I often put her to work holding instruments for me during surgeries, like she is seen here, helping me treat the paw of a lion. I enjoyed having her ride with me; I readily accepted her advice and help. She inspired me to write this book and for that I will be eternally grateful.

In closing, I would like to thank Brian, Tom, and Mickey Hunt,

Linda helping treat a lion's paw.

owners and operators of International Animal Exchange, for hiring me and entrusting me with the care of the wildlife held in their parks. I feel that the entire animal world owes the Hunts a debt of gratitude for having the foresight to become the pioneers of the open, drive-through wild animal park concept that ultimately led to much happier and healthier animals, which in turn led to more natural breeding. Their ideas about larger parks and zoos are still used today, resulting in a much more natural environment in which animals can survive.

Utilizing their animals in all of their parks in the United States, the Hunts have been able to ship many of their surplus exotics to zoos all over the world. They also have served as consultants to other countries regarding the construction of their zoos and parks. With wildlife conservation as their Number One priority, the Hunts have established such programs as Arabian oryx relocation, white tiger breeding, cheetah reproduction, Bongo breeding, African elephant relocation, and white rhino breeding, just to mention a few. It is their belief, as mine, that we are the keepers of our cherished wildlife, and it is up to us to do everything in our power to prevent the extinction of any species. I believe that animals were put on earth for man to care for and to learn from.

I will have to say that the lessons I learned from animals during my many years of being a practicing veterinarian have had a greater impact on my life than anything else. The beauty and intelligence of all animals has left me with no doubt that there is an almighty God who created each and every creature. I believe that God put animals on this earth not only for our enjoyment, but to serve as a guiding light and a constant reminder of what is good and pure in this world.